1-2-3® Spreadsheet Design

John M. Nevison

Brady
New York

 **BRADY**

Simon & Schuster, Inc.
Gulf+Western Building
One Gulf+Western Plaza
New York, NY 10023

DISTRIBUTED BY PRENTICE HALL TRADE

Manufactured in the United States of America

10 9 8 7 6 5 4 3 2 1

Library of Congress Cataloging-in-Publication Data

Nevison, John M.
    1-2-3 Spreadsheet Design / John M. Nevison
       p. cm.
    Includes index
    ISBN   0-13-838160-7 : $21.95
    1. Lotus 1-2-3 (Computer program) 2. Business—Data processing.
3. Electronic spreadsheets. I. Title. II. Title: One-two-three
spreadsheet design.
HF5548.4.L67N46 1989
005.36'9—dc20   89-9827
                                             CIP

Again to Susannah, Laura, and Nancy

Contents

Acknowledgments

The ideas that began the journey toward this book arose in discussions with John Kenower, Timothy Stein and Julie Bingham. The ideas were given their first field tests in courses at CIGNA Corporation and at the Boston Edison Company. Students contributed ideas in other classes taught at Arco, CBS, Chesebrough-Ponds, Coca-Cola, GTE, Gillette, General Electric, Lotus, Melon Bank, and Westinghouse. The manuscript profited from the careful reading of Jim Chelini, Joe Gwinn, Bill Schillhammer, Steve Shapse, and Tim Stein. Michael Vitale of the Harvard Business School (now of Prudential) and Ted Standish of the Gillette Company had kind words when they were needed most. Elva Wohlers generously extended the "two week" loan of her Compaq computer to several months. Scott Tucker of Lotus provided a critical look at Release 3 that made a big difference to several ideas in this version. Michael O'Brien gave the manuscript the critical reading it needed (and a new rule, Test and Edit). Milissa Koloski of Brady, has unwaveringly supported this book and efforts to get it to the retail reader. My two daughters, Laura and Susannah, provided necessary hugs when needed. My final and largest debt of gratitude is to my wife, Nancy Ross McJennett, who assumed the extra family responsibilities that allowed me the luxury of this work. The mistakes that remain are unavoidably the responsibility of the author.

John M. Nevison
Concord, MA

Limits of Liability and Disclaimer of Warranty

The Author and publisher of this book have used their best efforts in preparing this book and the programs contained in it. These efforts include the development, research, and testing of the theories and programs to determine their effectiveness. The author and publisher make no warranty of any kind, expressed or implied, with regard to these programs or the documentation contained in this book. The author and publisher shall not be liable in any event for incidental or consequential damages in connection with or arising out of, the furnishing, performance, or use of these programs.

Trademarks

The names 1-2-3, Symphony, and Jazz are a registered trademarks of Lotus Development Corporation.

Preface

Writing a good spreadsheet requires the kind of careful thought you would devote to writing a good letter. Editing either document demands further patient attention. The purpose of this small book is to help you write and edit a spreadsheet. Will Strunk once wrote a book on how to write clear English. E. B. White added a section on style and republished the book as *The Elements of Style*. This book takes its inspiration from that book.

The rules are short, the discussion is limited, and the examples are simple in the hope that the ideas will be easy to read and reread.

The Need for Rules of Style

The need for these rules of style is larger than the technology. A word processor cannot make a good writer, nor can 1-2-3 make a sound analyst. There is no technological fix for sloppy thought or poor expression. You need to know that writing a good spreadsheet is hard work, that this work can be rewarding and fulfilling, and that the rules of style in this book can help you to do this work well.

These 22 rules are not intended to set brittle standards of performance. They are intended to encourage you, the spreadsheet author, to think seriously about the purpose of your work. All spreadsheets must first be correct. If they are to maintain this correctness over time they must be clear. If they are to maintain this correctness when they are modified by others, they must be clear and well structured.

If these rules help you form the habits of careful spreadsheet construction, of reflection and revision, of precision and focus, they will dramatically enhance your professional productivity.

The examples that accompany the rules show weak and strong versions of the ideas in practice. The terms "weak" and "strong" were chosen to indicate that these are merely examples on a continuum: Examples can be worse than the weak and better than the strong. As you work on your spreadsheets you very well may improve on the examples provided here.

Novice Reader, Experienced Reader

If you are new to spreadsheets, before you use this book you must learn 1-2-3. You must know how to build and copy formulas, how to move areas about on the spreadsheet, and how to make graphs. You may find parts of this book helpful without knowing 1-2-3, but you will want to read the rules again after you have mastered it. In short, you should know something about your paints and brushes before you begin to explore the problems of composing a picture.

As a novice spreadsheet user, please **follow the rule before you break it**. After you use an apparently inconvenient rule on a few spreadsheets, you may find it has become an absolute necessity. You may also find that because you do not have to unlearn a lot of bad habits your work may quickly achieve a higher standard than that of your more experienced colleagues.

If you are an experienced user of spreadsheets you may have difficulty with some of the rules in this book. However, if you strongly disagree with a rule it should be for the same reason that the rule was advanced: There is a better way to build a clear, correct spreadsheet. Few, if any, experienced readers will agree with all of the rules, but every experienced reader will find at least one new rule that will improve his or her spreadsheets. That one rule will repay the cost of the book and the effort to read it.

As all readers become experienced they should heed the other unwritten rule: **When you have a good reason, break the rule.** These rules should encourage thoughtful activity, not blind obedience.

Particular 1-2-3 Versions

The spreadsheets in this book will run as shown in 1-2-3 Release 1A and higher. Some of the typeface conventions will require Allways or Release 3. Every spreadsheet function that appears here is available in 1-2-3. The features that support graphing may require special software products to appear exactly as they do in the text.

NOTE WELL: Some of the graphs in this book were created by hand editing 1-2-3 graphs. Do **not** try to blindly reproduce the charts and graphs as they appear in the text.

The macros will work in Release 1A and some have been rewritten for Release 2 and beyond.

Spreadsheets as Tools

This book extends its predecessor, *The Elements of Spreadsheet Style*, (Brady, 1987) by expanding the number of working spreadsheets to more than 30. In order to make these tools accessible they have been cross-referenced extensively in the Appendices. The general categories of tool are illustrated in the following diagram.

The Business Spreadsheet Toolkit

Management Tools	
Financial Tools	Strategic Business Tools
Personal Business Tools	
Other Spreadsheet Tools	

So in addition to learning more about spreadsheet construction, you can use the examples in this book to construct a considerable variety of personal spreadsheet tools.

Nursery Rhymes

The nursery rhymes in the book are intended to relieve the somewhat sober nature of the subject. Rhymes that are puzzles introduce some of the chapters. Rhymes that are about historical personages appear in the text and have dates that loosely correspond to the character about whom the rhyme was written. For example, in the spreadsheet SIXPENCE, the King is Henry the Eighth, the Queen is Catherine of Aragon, the maid is Anne Boleyn (who eventually had her head, not just her nose, snapped off), and the blackbird is

Cardinal Wolsey; the date is 1536, an arbitrary year during the reign of Henry the Eighth. Mary, Queen of Scots, figures in several rhymes, and so does Queen Elizabeth the first. Other English royalty can be guessed by the dates. For those who like historical puzzles, Humpty Dumpty's spreadsheet contains the only specific historical date in the book. The date on the spreadsheets ascribed to Mother Goose herself (she has no known tie to an historical personage) is 1386, the year when Chaucer is believed to have begun his *Canterbury Tales*.

1

Introduction: Form Follows Function

FINGERS AND TOES
Every lady in this land
Has twenty nails, upon each hand
Five, and twenty on hands and feet:
All this is true, without deceit.

A spreadsheet should be of good character. It should be straightforward to build, easy to read, simple to use, receptive to change, and, above all, free of error.

The first step toward achieving this goal is to construct a spreadsheet that has an appropriate form. This form is the cornerstone of correctness. When each function is carried out in an appropriate location, its activity can be verified by eye and reviewed by a thoughtful reader. The appropriate form also denies errors a place to hide. When something is out of place, it looks out of place.

Because the appropriate form focuses your attention on the proper detail at the proper place, it is easy to remember and you do not get lost. A user engaged in the small changes of normal use knows where to alter an initial "what if" assumption, where to slip in a new calculation, and where to modify a printed report.

When a spreadsheet must undergo a major overhaul to meet a new need, the appropriate form will suggest where you can make the additions and deletions.

Finally, the appropriate form not only reveals the completed thought, it supports and guides the unfolding thought. A completed spreadsheet often can be reused as a template for subsequent work. Such a template saves a significant amount of start-up time on a new project, ensures that you will not forget an important section of the spreadsheet, and provides a guiding framework for thinking about the problem under examination.

A Song of Sixpence

To understand what this appropriate form might look like in practice, consider the spreadsheet model below. While it is small, it raises several questions. Who wrote it? What is its name? When was it written? What is its purpose? Why is it so hard to read? Is it complete? Is it accurate?

	A	B	C	D	E	F
1		Income	Rent	Tax	Poor tax	Real inc.
2	King	90000	15000	20700	180	54120
3	Queen	75000	12000	17250	180	45570
4	Maid	12000	1000	2760	180	8060
5	Blackbird	3000	200	690	180	1930
6	Totals	180000	28200	41400	720	109680

Now take a look at a second version of the same model.

	A	B	C	D	E	F
1	Twopence	10 December 1536	King Henry			
2						
3	To show how income is distributed in the kingdom.					
4						
5		KINGDOM INCOME DISTRIBUTION 1537				
6						
7	Person	Income	Rent	Tax	Poor tax	Real inc.
8						
9	King	90,000	15,000	20,700	180	54,120
10	Queen	75,000	12,000	17,250	180	45,570
11	Maid	12,000	1,000	2,760	180	8,060
12	Blackbird	3,000	200	690	180	1,930
13		-------------	-------------	-------------	-------------	-------------
14	Totals	180,000	28,200	41,400	720	109,680

Twopence is a clear improvement. You know its name, when it was created, and by whom. You have been thrust into a nursery rhyme kingdom. You know the model's purpose: to show how income is distributed in the kingdom. The results have been laid out in an easy-to-read fashion. You have some idea how this model might be used.

Yet this apparently complete version is not complete. Twopence is hiding information. While you expect a spreadsheet to work with formulas you can't see (for example, the Totals row or the Real Income column), you do not want formulas to contain hidden numbers. Hidden numbers are buried threats. Unknown to the viewer, and hard to find for the user, these surreptitious figures can sabotage the best intentioned effort. In the case of Twopence the hidden number is the tax rate that is buried in the formulas in the Tax column. You are being denied access to important information about this model. The third version reveals this small, but highly significant, detail.

	A	B	C	D	E	F
1	THRPENCE (Threepence)		10 December 1536		King Henry	
2						
3	To show how income is distributed in the kingdom.					
4						
5	Assumptions:		23% Tax rate			
6			180 Poor tax			
7	Model:					
8		KINGDOM INCOME DISTRIBUTION 1537				
9						
10	Person	Income	Rent	Tax	Poor tax	Real inc.
11						
12	King	90,000	15,000	20,700	180	54,120
13	Queen	75,000	12,000	17,250	180	45,570
14	Maid	12,000	1,000	2,760	180	8,060
15	Blackbird	3,000	200	690	180	1,930
16		----------	----------	----------	----------	----------
17	Totals	180,000	28,200	41,400	720	109,680

Threepence tells you that the tax rate is 23 percent. Now what you see is what you get. All of the information on which the model depends is visible.

Notice that the Poor Tax appears as an assumption, too. While it was visible before, it was repeated four times. Now, by appearing as an assumption and having the four occurrences in the model all tied to the assumption, the Poor Tax may be changed by changing only one number instead of four.

You can also change the tax rate for the whole model by changing one number, the 23 percent at the top of the model. In addition to making the information accessible, the visible assumptions allow you to modify the program without digging into the formulas.

For many purposes Threepence may be satisfactory. However, if King Henry knows he will be off on a quest and wants to leave things in a fashion that will be easy for Queen Mary to handle, he might rearrange the model for another person to use.

	A	B	C	D	E	F
1	FORPENCE (Fourpence)		10 December 1536		King Henry	
2						
3	To show how income is distributed in the kingdom					
4	--					
5	Initial data and beginning assumptions					
6		23%	Tax rate			
7		180	Poor tax			
8						
9		Income	Person	Rent	Dwelling	
10		90000	King	15000	Counting House	
11		75000	Queen	12000	Parlor	
12		12000	Maid	1000	Garden house	
13		3000	Blackbird	200	Garden	
14	--					
15	Income distribution model					
16		KINGDOM INCOME DISTRIBUTION 1537				
17						
18	Person	Income	Rent	Tax	Poor tax	Real inc.
19						
20	King	90,000	15,000	20,700	180	54,120
21	Queen	75,000	12,000	17,250	180	45,570
22	Maid	12,000	1,000	2,760	180	8,060
23	Blackbird	3,000	200	690	180	1,930
24		-----------	-----------	-----------	-----------	-----------
25	Totals	180,000	28,200	41,400	720	109,680
26	===					

Fourpence extracts all the raw numbers from the model, collects them, and labels them in the initial data area near the top of the spreadsheet. Fourpence changes all the numbers in the model area to formulas. For example, the King's 90,000 income in the model is no longer a number; it is a one-term formula that refers to the raw value in the initial data. All the apparent numbers in the model are formulas that refer to the raw values in the initial data or formulas that construct other values, such as the tax, from these numbers. Fourpence separates all the raw data from the formulas.

Having this separation allows a split in how the model is handled. The original author, the King, can work anywhere in the spreadsheet. But when he is finished, he can lock up the formulas in the model itself. The second user of the model, the Queen, never has to touch a formula. She may exercise the model by simply changing figures in the initial data. Providing an area for the initial data allows the raw data to be not only visible, but fully labeled. In this case, you find out that the parlor rents for $12,000 and you can infer that the Queen is in the parlor (eating bread and honey).

The King wants to prepare some clear, concise reports: one for the Queen on the spending of the royal funds and one for the maid on the distribution of the royal burden. He extends his model to include these two reports.

	A	B	C	D	E	F	G
1	FIVPENCE (Fivepence) 10 December 1536 King Henry						
2							
3	To show how income is distributed in the kingdom						
4							
5	Contents:						
6	INTRO	Introduction: Title, description, contents					
7	INITIAL	Initial data and beginning assumptions					
8	MODEL	Income distribution model					
9	REPORT1	Report on kingdom's spending for the year					
10	REPORT2	Distribution of royal burden					
11							
12	--						
13	Initial data and beginning assumptions						
14		23%	Tax rate				
15		180	Poor tax				
16		1537	Year of report				
17							
18		Income	Person		Rent	Dwelling	
19		90000	King		15000	Counting House	
20		75000	Queen		12000	Parlor	
21		12000	Maid		1000	Garden house	
22		3000	Blackbird		200	Garden	
23	--						
24	Income distribution model						
25		KINGDOM INCOME DISTRIBUTION				1537	
26							
27	Person	Income	Rent	Tax	Poor tax	Real inc.	
28							
29	King	90,000	15,000	20,700	180	54,120	
30	Queen	75,000	12,000	17,250	180	45,570	
31	Maid	12,000	1,000	2,760	180	8,060	
32	Blackbird	3,000	200	690	180	1,930	
33		---------------	---------------	---------------	---------------	---------------	
34	Totals	180,000	28,200	41,400	720	109,680	
35	--						

(continued)

	A	B	C	D	E	F	G
36	Report on kingdom's spending for the year					1537	
37							
38		28,200	Funds for the maintenance of the buildings and grounds.				
39		41,400	Funds for the defense of the kingdom				
40		720	Funds for the poor				
41		---------------					
42		70,320	Total spent				
43	---						
44	Distribution of royal burden			1537			
45							
46		Person	Burden	Burden as percentage of income			
47			$	%			
48		King	35,880	40			
49		Queen	29,430	39			
50		Maid	3,940	33			
51		Blackbird	1,070	36			
52			---------------	---------------			
53			70,320	39			
54	==						

Now that the model has grown beyond what can be seen on one screen, the King has added a table of contents. The contents gives the reader a quick idea of the full extent of the model. The King also has added two new regions to the spreadsheet. Each region is intended to be a report that can be printed out independently of the rest of the model. By giving each report its own area the King has made it easier for either report to be modified. Because he wanted the year to appear in both reports as well as in his original model, he has added the year of the report to the initial data.

Looking at Fivepence you might wonder whether the whole effort has been overdone. Clearly, this model is more work than the already satisfactory Threepence. Is Fivepence worth the trouble? To answer this question, consider for a moment how it might be used.

Late in 1537 the King was away on a quest and he wrote home to the queen suggesting that they increase the tax rate to whatever was necessary to cover an anticipated $50,000 expense in the defense of the Kingdom. The rye crop had been good, so the Queen knew everyone would receive an increase in their income. The Queen wanted to increase the poor tax, if she could do it without increasing the overall royal burden on the population.

The Queen called up Fivepence and:

1. Entered the new incomes: $100,000 for the king, $88,000 for the Queen, $15,000 for the Maid, and $4,500 for the Blackbird.

2. Held rents the same.

3. Increased the tax rate until the total tax exceeded $50,000.

4. Increased the poor tax until the overall burden equalled the previous year's burden.

When she was finished, she retitled the model Sixpence.

	A	B	C	D	E	F	G
1	Sixpence	15 November 1537	Queen Mary				
2							
3	To show how income is distributed in the kingdom						
4							
5	Contents:						
6	INTRO	Introduction: Title, description, contents					
7	INITIAL	Initial data and beginning assumptions					
8	MODEL	Income distribution model					
9	REPORT1	Report on kingdom's spending for the year					
10	REPORT2	Distribution of royal burden					
11							
12	---						
13	Initial data and beginning assumptions						
14		25%	Tax rate				
15		471	Poor tax				
16		1538	Year of report				
17							
18		Income	Person		Rent	Dwelling	
19		100000	King		15000	Counting House	
20		88000	Queen		12000	Parlor	
21		15000	Maid		1000	Garden house	
22		4500	Blackbird		200	Garden	
23	---						

(continued)

	A	B	C	D	E	F	G
24	Income distribution model						
25		KINGDOM INCOME DISTRIBUTION				1538	
26							
27	Person	Income	Rent	Tax	Poor tax	Real inc.	
28							
29	King	100,000	15,000	25,000	471	59,529	
30	Queen	88,000	12,000	22,000	471	53,529	
31	Maid	15,000	1,000	3,750	471	9,779	
32	Blackbird	4,500	200	1,125	471	2,704	
33		------------	------------	------------	------------	------------	
34	Totals	207,500	28,200	51,875	1,884	125,541	
35							
36	Report on kingdom's spending for the year				1538		
37							
38		28,200	Funds for the maintenance of the buildings and grounds.				
39		51,875	Funds for the defense of the kingdom				
40		1,884	Funds for the poor				
41		------------					
42		81,959	Total spent				
43							
44	Distribution of royal burden			1538			
45							
46		Person	Burden	Burden as percentage of income			
47			$	%			
48		King	40,471	40			
49		Queen	34,471	39			
50		Maid	5,221	35			
51		Blackbird	1,796	40			
52			------------	------------			
53			81,959	39			
54		==					

Because the structure of Fivepence made it convenient for a second person to use, the model was successfully integrated into the regular work habits of the administration. If the King set out to build a model to help rule the kingdom, he achieved his goal. The Queen could carry on in the King's absence.

What is the moral of these six versions? Form follows function. What form is appropriate depends on what function the spreadsheet is intended to fulfill. This moral does not mean all forms are adequate to some purpose. Onepence and Twopence are clearly unsatisfactory. Threepence, Fourpence, and Fivepence, however, each satisfy a different purpose. If you wish to have a personal model you can quickly build and change, then Threepence is fine. If you are going to let another person use your model, Fourpence is a sound approach. If you find that your model is composed of several parts, Fivepence is appropriate. Sixpence is evidence that Fivepence works.

To understand in more detail how spreadsheets should be fashioned, you need to know the rules for the basic form and the rules for extensions to the basic form. With these rules you can fashion forms appropriate to your functions. The next four chapters will present these 22 rules.

2

The Basic Form

AN EQUAL
Read my riddle, I pray.
What God never sees,
What the king seldom sees,
What we see every day.

The basic form divides into three fundamental parts: (1) the Introduction, where you tell the reader what is about to appear; (2) the Initial Data Area, where you present the raw material of the model; and (3) the Model Area, where the spreadsheet performs its work in an informative and attractive manner. Even a spreadsheet that ends up omitting or abbreviating one part should begin with a plan that includes all three.

Introduction

Make a Formal Introduction

The top of the model introduces the reader to the model. The reader must get his bearings here, and the work of the spreadsheet is fit into larger contexts. The top ties the model to the outside world. Several devices play introductory roles:

- The title line telegraphs critical information.

- The description declares the purpose.

- The directions say how to use the model.

- The references offer collateral information.

- The table of contents maps the spreadsheet's organization.

By the time the reader leaves the introduction he should have a good idea how the model fits into the activities of the real world and where to go in the model to explore the details.

Title to Tell

The first thing the reader encounters is the title of the model. Make it tell. It should be short, apt, and memorable. In conjunction with the first few lines of the introduction, the title should allow the reader to decide whether to quit or to continue. All of the remaining reading will be colored by the title's first impression. Make sure it is the right impression.

Weak	*Strong*		
Sim3x5	Pies	4 March 1620	S. Simon
Tuff13.6	Tuffet	15 May 1560	M. Muffet
Lost	Sheep	22 June 1563	B. Peep

The title line telegraphs critical information. A strong title line contains at least the name of the model, the date it was completed, and the person who wrote it. Plain names are more informative than abbreviations. Nouns or verbs tell more than adjectives.

Choosing the right name for your model is especially important when your model will immediately become the property of several people or must fit into an existing scheme of documents. Others can immediately identify how your contribution fits into the group effort if the name follows the local convention. Suppose your model is the third one supporting a proposal to Acorn Corporation. You might want the title to be:

Acorn Proposal #33 Model #3

But if it must fit in eight characters on an IBM PC, it requires some abbreviation. Here is what one standard might look like:

Weak	*Strong*
ACP33M03	ACP33M03 (Acorn Corporation Proposal 33, Model 3)
	24 May 1488 T. Tucker

Terse titles that follow an established abbreviation standard need a de-coded explanation in the spreadsheet itself. The strong example shows how a two-line title can meet a terse naming standard and yet remain comprehensible to a busy reader. Naming conventions also need the support of:

- A list of the current conventions posted on the wall near every computer that will use these names,

- A regular, attentive review and update procedure,

- A manager (called a librarian) to oversee the function.

A very useful bit of information to have along with the title is the date the current copy was printed. You may add this to your spreadsheet using the @TODAY function or, for Release 2.01 and later, the @NOW function and the label ": Date Printed."

Weak   *Strong*

Sheep   22 June 1563   B. Peep   Sheep   22 June 1563   B. Peep
                                                  12-Dec-88 : Date Printed

The strong title area tells you that while the spreadsheet was written a long time ago, the copy you are reading was printed rather recently. The date printed warns you to be on the lookout for undocumented revisions.

There is no magic in having only one or two lines for the title. When the critical information grows to several lines to meet work demands, the title line can become a title area. The title area should be so familiar that it can be read like a title line. The title, line or area, should telegraph critical information.

Strong

	A	B	C	D
1	NURSERY KINGDOM CONFIDENTIAL INFORMATION			
2				
3	Name:	SILBELL (Silver Bells)		
4	Date:	12 August 1560		
5	Author:	M. Contrary		
6	Dept:	Garden		
7	Division:	Outdoor		
8	Date Printed:	16-Feb-89		
9				
10	Date last modified:	23 Sept 1561		
11	Last modified by:	M. Contrary		

Several critical pieces of information appear in Silver Bells. The formal heading identifies the owner of the information and notifies the reader that this information is confidential. Not only do you have the name, date, and author, you know the department name, the division name, and the name of the corporation. On August 12, 1560, Mary Contrary completed the spreadsheet Silver Bells while she was in the Garden Department of the Outdoor Division of the Nursery Kingdom.

A modification is also mentioned here. You know that Mary Contrary revised the model on September 23, 1561. Another style of doing the revision history could allow for the insertion of further updates.

Strong

	A	B	C	D	E	F
1	NURSERY KINGDOM CONFIDENTIAL INFORMATION					
2						
3	Name:	SILBELL2 (Silver Bells Number 2)				
4	Date:	12 August 1560				
5	Author:	M. Contrary				
6	Dept:	Garden				
7	Division:	Outdoor				
8	Date printed:	16-Feb-89				
9						
10	Date modified	Who modified and what				
11						
12	4 Nov 1561	M. Contrary added a row for pretty maids				
13	23 Sept 1561	M. Contrary added a column for cockleshells				

This modification format allows the reader to read the history of changes to the original spreadsheet. You can see that Mary most recently added a row for pretty maids and before that a column of cockleshells. If the spreadsheet starts to misbehave when you use it, you have some strong hints where to begin looking for recently introduced errors. When the modification history grows unwieldy, you should write a new version of the spreadsheet and revise the entire introduction.

Declare the Model's Purpose

The model's purpose should be immediately available to the reader. He needs to know that his purposes and the spreadsheet's are similar. After the reader knows what the model intends to achieve, he needs to have some idea how the model will achieve it. This does not require a lengthy description, just a clear one. The model's intentions should be honorable and clearly stated.

Weak	*Strong*
Set of accounts on the King's travels.	The purpose of this model is to maintain a set of accounts on the King's travels.
Accounts receivable.	Manage accounts receivable by recording transactions and printing summary reports.
Expense reports.	This spreadsheet will print the Queen's travel expense reports.

One hallmark of a strong description is a telling verb, an action word that conveys the activity of the model. The right verb animates the description and quickly conveys the model's purpose. The phrase "The purpose of this model is" leaves no question in the reader's mind about the model's goal.

Weak	*Strong*
Add all the tasks' means and variances and compute the project's mean and variance.	Estimate the length of a project that consists of several tasks.
	Add all the tasks' means and variances and compute the project's mean and variance.

First describe the goal, then how to achieve it. Only if the reader wants to estimate a project's length is he interested in the method. The weak version makes a good second line in the strong version. Answer "What?" before "How?" Be sure everyone has agreed on the mountain before you set out to climb it.

Strong

<table>
<tr><td></td><td>A</td><td>B</td><td>C</td><td>D</td><td>E</td><td>F</td></tr>
<tr><td>1</td><td colspan="6">SMALLNEW   17 July 1386   Mother Goose</td></tr>
<tr><td>2</td><td colspan="6"></td></tr>
<tr><td>3</td><td colspan="6">Provide a framework with which to begin building models.</td></tr>
<tr><td>4</td><td colspan="6"></td></tr>
<tr><td>5</td><td colspan="6">To use: Call it up, change its name, save it with its new name,</td></tr>
<tr><td>6</td><td colspan="6">and edit to your purpose.</td></tr>
<tr><td>7</td><td colspan="6">--------------- ---------------- --------------- --------------- --------------- ---------------</td></tr>
<tr><td>8</td><td colspan="6">Initial Data:</td></tr>
<tr><td>9</td><td colspan="6">   Goes here</td></tr>
<tr><td>10</td><td colspan="6">--------------- ---------------- --------------- --------------- --------------- ---------------</td></tr>
<tr><td>11</td><td colspan="6">Model</td></tr>
<tr><td>12</td><td colspan="6">   Goes here</td></tr>
<tr><td>13</td><td colspan="6">--------------- ---------------- --------------- --------------- --------------- ---------------</td></tr>
</table>

Here you see a model devoid of content, yet with a description that serves a purpose. The description succinctly tells what SMALLNEW's purpose is: to provide a framework with which to begin building models. This is a startup model that you can use to make other models. This simple template saves your having to think about how to organize your work. It allows you to begin by editing rather than writing.

Give Clear Instructions

Just as the initial description bridges the gap between the model and the outside world, clear instructions can bridge the gap between the reader of the model and its user. Some who work with a model will only read a paper copy. Others will see it in operation on a computer screen. The description may satisfy the reader, but often the user needs instructions. A step-by-step numbered list is an excellent way to give clear instructions.

Weak

<table>
<tr><td></td><td>A</td><td>B</td><td>C</td><td>D</td><td>E</td><td>F</td><td>G</td></tr>
<tr><td>5</td><td colspan="7">Directions. Correct the status of the sheep. Group all the lost sheep together.</td></tr>
<tr><td>6</td><td colspan="7">Revise the COUNT and SUM functions in the model. Call up the pie</td></tr>
<tr><td>7</td><td colspan="7">chart entitled SHEEP'S PIE.</td></tr>
</table>

Strong

	A	B	C	D	E	F
16	Directions:					
17						
18	1. Correct the "lost" and "found" status of the sheep in the initial data.					
19	2. Sort the initial data to group all the lost sheep together.					
20	3. Revise the COUNT functions under "Number" in the model to count					
21	the two groups of lost and found.					
22	4. Revise the SUM functions under "Value" in the model to sum					
23	the value of the two groups of lost and found.					
24	5. Call up pie chart entitled SHEEP'S PIE.					

The weak and strong examples differ in two important aspects. The obvious aspect is that the strong version is a numbered list. The numbers explicitly order the steps and make it easy for a user to check off each step as it is completed. The subtle aspect is that the weak version is not as clear as it should be. The weak version is a first draft. After you write instructions, be sure to let someone else try to follow them. Such a trial will show you whether the directions are adequate and, if not, how they can be improved. The strong version is a revised draft that was written after readers had trouble following the weak version.

Here is another set of directions taken completely out of context:

Strong

	A	B	C	D	E	F	G
18	Directions:						
19	In the initial data area:						
20	1. State the decision and the desired result.						
21	2. Put in choices and make comments.						
22	3. Enter "must" objectives—things that must be satisfied.						
23	4. Enter "want" objectives—things that you would like to have.						
24	5. Weight the importance of the "want" objectives and comment.						
25	6. Rate or rank the choices against each objective.						
26	For example, rate the best choice (of four) as 4 and let the others have 3,						
27	2, or 1. You may have ties if you wish. You may rate a choice 0 if you wish.						
28	In the decision model:						
29	7. Examine the model's results and graph.						
30	8. Revise and reexamine the importance of objectives, the rank of choices,						
31	and other features to be sure of your choice.						
32	9. List the adverse consequences of the best choice to see if it will work.						

Notice that these instructions can stand by themselves. Even without their model they make a certain amount of sense. They are broken into pieces that make it easier for the user to locate where to do which steps. The directions are further clarified in the actual model by a working example that illustrates where within the area to do each step.

A long list of instructions raises the question of where to place it. Frequently, just before the initial data area is a convenient spot. Sometimes, however, the user's needs are best served by including instructions nearer the point where they will be used. In a large model with many pieces, this means that the directions will be moved from the top of the model out to the part of the model where the user will be working. (See discussion of sub-models in Chapter 5.) If significant instructions have been moved, leave a note to that effect in the description at the top.

Strong

Instructions on how to use the Monte Carlo portion of the model appear there.

The user can quickly see that the additional support will be available on the Monte Carlo method near its use in the model.

Beyond instructions for the user, more detailed explanation about the ideas behind the model are sometimes necessary to ensure a full understanding of the extent and limitations of the model.

Reference Critical Ideas

Reference in the strong sense. Provide a full, accurate guide to the journal, book, or professional communication where the idea originated. Santayana cautioned "Those who cannot remember the past are condemned to repeat it." Many ideas in a model are original and some borrowed ideas are too simple to bear mention, but an important idea should reveal its past. If it is incorrect, the reader must be given a chance to discover the source of the error. Sometimes an enterprising reader will spot an idea, follow the reference back to the source, and work forward to compose a model tailored to his or her special needs. Do not deny the reader this link to the past.

Strong

Reference: The Real Mother Goose, Chicago, IL: Rand McNally, 1916.

Reference: Thomas, Katherine Elwes, The Real Personages of Mother Goose, Boston, MA: Lonthrop, Lee & Shepard Co, 1930.

Reference: Kepner, Charles H., and Tregoe, Benjamin B., The New Rational Manager, Princeton, NJ: Princeton Research Press, 1981.

Reference: Nevison, John M., The Little Book of BASIC Style: How to Write a Program You Can Read, Reading, MA: Addison-Wesley, 1978.

Reference: See Materials Handling Procedure Manual, Document Number A34.77, Rev. 3.6, pp. 64-68.

Reference: If you have any questions, call Bo Peep at extension 3456.

A reference need not be only to a book. A knowledgeable individual, a file with the related information, a standard form the organization has been using for years; each can be an appropriate reference in certain circumstances.

Map the Contents

The underlying organization of a spreadsheet is spatial. Geography is all. To let the reader know where things are requires a map. One of the most convenient maps is a table of contents. If the sections of your model are kept to the left and stacked vertically, the table of contents can be an accurate map to the location of each part of the model.

A table of contents is the last part of the introduction in all but the smallest spreadsheets. As soon as the spreadsheet slips off the screen and escapes your visual span of control you will need a table of contents to see where you are.

Strong

	A	B	C	D	E
1	NINPENCE (Ninepence)		10 December 1536	King Henry	
2					
3	To show how income is distributed in the kingdom				
4					
5	Contents:				
6		Introduction: Title, description, contents			
7		Initial data and beginning assumptions			
8		Income distribution model			
9		Report on kingdom's spending for the year			
10		Report on distribution of royal burden			
11		Data for pie chart of burden			

A table of contents is a powerful organizer for a reader. If the reader is only concerned with the spending report, she can focus her attention on it at once. But if she wishes to know more about the data that led to the graphs, she knows where to look.

The name in the table of contents should correspond to the name in that area of the spreadsheet.

Strong

Contents
    Initial Data
    Finance Model
    Quarterly Sales Report
    Pie Chart Data

Initial Data

Finance Model

Quarterly Sales Report
Pie Chart Data

You can name the areas of the spreadsheet with Range Names and display them in the table of contents to keep them visible. When you do this you may jump to any area with a very few keystrokes (the GoTo key, the Name key, and select the name of the range you wish to jump to).

Strong

	A	B	C	D	E
1	TENPENCE	10 December 1536	King Henry		
2	16-Feb-89	: Date printed			
3					
4	To show how income is distributed in the kingdom				
5					
6	Contents: (each section is a named range)				
7	INTRO	Introduction: Title, description, contents			
8	INITIAL	Initial data and beginning assumptions			
9	MODEL	Income distribution model			
10	REPORT1	Report on kingdom's spending for the year			
11	REPORT2	Report on distribution of royal burden			
12	GRAPH	Data for pie chart of burden			

Here the named range is on the left and a larger explanation appears on the right. TENPENCE gives the user an extra reason to be interested in the table of contents: By using the named ranges, the user can jump to the right place in the spreadsheet. Type the GoTo and the Name key, select the <range name>. Named ranges also avoid the annoying problem of using cell locations that must be changed every time the spreadsheet is rearranged. The reader of a printed version of the model welcomes the extra information about the organization of the spreadsheet.

Strong

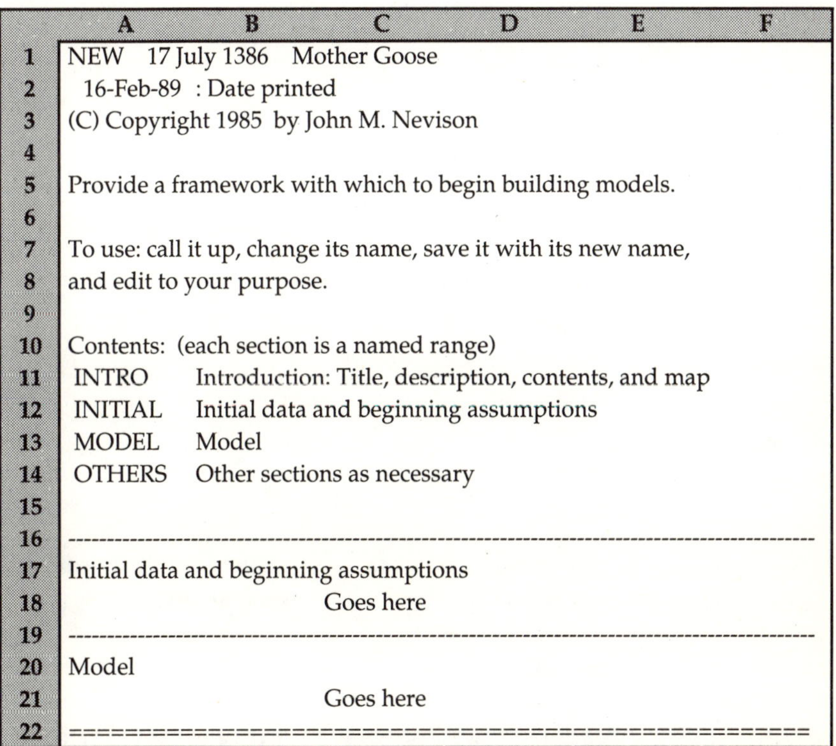

	A	B	C	D	E	F
1	NEW 17 July 1386 Mother Goose					
2	16-Feb-89 : Date printed					
3	(C) Copyright 1985 by John M. Nevison					
4						
5	Provide a framework with which to begin building models.					
6						
7	To use: call it up, change its name, save it with its new name,					
8	and edit to your purpose.					
9						
10	Contents: (each section is a named range)					
11	INTRO Introduction: Title, description, contents, and map					
12	INITIAL Initial data and beginning assumptions					
13	MODEL Model					
14	OTHERS Other sections as necessary					
15						
16	--					
17	Initial data and beginning assumptions					
18	Goes here					
19	--					
20	Model					
21	Goes here					
22	==					

This template, NEW, extends the template SMALLNEW by including a table of contents. NEW is the common starting place for most of the spreadsheets in this book. The already named ranges give the user a head start with the work.

Sometimes a model's geography has horizontal spread as well as vertical depth. If so, include a map beneath the table of contents.

Weak

Contents
North America
Europe
Asia
South America
Africa
Australia
Antarctica

Strong

Contents
North America
Europe
Asia
South America
Africa
Australia
Antarctica

Map

North America	Europe	Asia
South America	Africa	
		Australia
Antarctica		

Weak

Contents
raw material purchases
payables
finished product orders
receivables
general ledger
payroll

Strong

Contents
raw material purchases
payables
finished product orders
receivables
general ledger
payroll

Map

raw material purchases	finished product orders
payables	receivables
general ledger	
payroll	

With the continents mapped, the user knows which way to travel with his cursor, and the reader knows which way to travel with his eye. The reader knows when to go down and when to go sideways. The raw materials and finished products are arranged in parallel. They feed the general ledger, which is below them. The payroll is a separate function below the general ledger.

The map tells the user where to safely insert rows and columns. The Australia section can have rows inserted in it without hitting Africa. The user knows at once where the lower right corner of the model is: below Antarctica to the right of Australia, below payroll and to the right of receivables.

Experienced users testify that a map is a powerful way to reclaim control over a spreadsheet that has gotten out of hand. The map organizes and informs. Sometimes it will even point out how to reorganize your model. It will always make your model easier to comprehend, to grasp as a whole. A map restores your visual span of control over even the largest spreadsheets.

Lotus 1-2-3 Release 3 includes pages of spreadsheets A, B, C, and so on. Each page has an upper left corner labeled A1, for example, A:A1, B:A1, and C:A1. You may use these pages to create a dynamic table of contents that looks like this:

Strong

A:	A	B	C	D	E
1	TENPENCE 10 December 1536 King Henry				
2	16-Feb-89 : Date printed				
3					
4	To show how income is distributed in the kingdom				
5					
6	Contents: (each section is a named range)				
7	+A:A1 Introduction: Title, description, contents				
8	+A:A15 Initial data and beginning assumptions				
9	+A:A27 Income distribution model				
10	+B:A1 Report on kingdom's spending for the year				
11	+C:A1 Report on distribution of royal burden				
12	+D:A1 Data for pie chart of burden				

In this example, the author created a dynamic reference to the appropriate area and page by setting up a column where there is a formula that points to the appropriate page; these pointing formulas are formatted as Range Format Text. This trick has the pleasing effect that if you later insert or delete a page, the references will adjust automatically and continue to point to the correct page.

If you know there will always be four pages, you could map the contents in the following way.

Strong

	A	B	C	D	E
1	TENPENCE	10 December 1536	King Henry		
2	16-Feb-89 : Date printed				
3					
4	To show how income is distributed in the kingdom				
5					
6	Contents: (each section is a named range)				
7					
8	Page A	Introduction: Title, description, contents			
9		Initial data and beginning assumptions			
10		Income distribution model			
11					
12	Page B	Report on kingdom's spending for the year			
13					
14	Page C	Report on distribution of royal burden			
15					
16	Page D	Data for pie chart of burden			

Beyond a sharp title, a clear purpose, good directions, helpful references, and a simple map, your introduction may include additional information. What you should add to the description depends on the function of the model, the knowledge of the reader, the skill of the user, and the framework of the organization within which the model will be used. (See Chapter 8 for more discussion of the organization.) Err on the side of overinforming your reader. He may not be stupid, but he is probably more ignorant than you suspect. Your introduction should include everything necessary to make a successful bridge from the model itself to the world in which it will be used.

After the spreadsheet has been thoroughly introduced, it must set to work to achieve its purpose. Good spreadsheet form is more architecture than interior design. The next rules define the second and third parts, the major architectural elements, of the basic form: the Initial Data Area and the Model Area. The spreadsheet's goal is to arrive clearly at the desired results. Each part serves this goal in its own way. The Initial Data Area stores the beginning material of the model, the raw data and the initial assumptions. The Model Area is where formulas manufacture consequences from the raw material. Here complex formulas are explained, intermediate terms appear, and final results are often displayed.

The Initial Data Area

Identify the Data

Data are the grist for the model's mill. They are numbers you know when you write the model. They may be three key constants or three thousand items in a database. They belong in their own area, where they may be clearly labeled and conveniently arranged. Such an area makes it easy for both the reader and user to identify the data. Without an Initial Data Area a weak model can be an unintended mystery.

Weak

	A	B	C	D	E	F	G
1	INFLATEA 1 January 1510 J. Horner						
2	16-Feb-89 : Date printed						
3	(C) Copyright 1983 John M. Nevison						
4							
5	Find the profit margin in an inflationary world where raw material						
6	costs, labor costs, and prices each grow at a different rate.						
7							
8	Growth Rate	1.03	1.15		1.07		
9							
10		Year	Raw mat	Labor	Total cst	Price	Profit	Margin
11		1510	56.00	21.00	77.00	100.00	23.00	23.00%
12		1511	57.68	24.15	81.83	107.00	25.17	23.52%
13		1512	59.41	27.77	87.18	114.49	27.31	23.85%
14		1513	61.19	31.94	93.13	122.50	29.37	23.98%
15		1514	63.03	36.73	99.76	131.08	31.32	23.90%
16		1515	64.92	42.24	107.16	140.26	33.10	23.60%

This weak example does not have an Initial Data Area. It is more puzzle than model. The model shows the profit of a product with different cost components growing at different rates. You see that a price increase of 7%—a 7% increase has a factor of 1.07—preserves profit margin. But you don't know with any certainty what the initial data are.

Strong

	A	B	C	D	E	F	G
1	INFLATEB 1 January 1510 J. Horner						
2	16-Feb-89 : Date printed						
3	(C) Copyright 1984 by John M. Nevison						
4							
5	Test pricing in an inflationary world where different costs						
6	growing at different rates affect the margin (% profit). By						
7	varying the price growth rate the user can attempt to preserve						
8	a certain margin in some future year.						
9							
10	Contents: (each section is a named range)						
11	INTRO Introductory material. title, description, and contents						
12	INIT Initial data						
13	MODEL Model						
14	---						
15	Initial Data:						
16			1510 Starting Year				
17							
18	Cost structure			Growth rates			
19		$56.00	Raw material cost		1.03	Raw material growth rate	
20		$21.00	Labor cost		1.15	Labor growth rate	
21	$100.00	Price			1.07	Price growth rate	
22	---						
23	Model						
24	YEAR	MATERIAL	LABOR	TOTL COST	PRICE	PROFIT	MARGIN
25							
26	1510	56.00	21.00	77.00	100.00	23.00	23.00%
27	1511	57.68	24.15	81.83	107.00	25.17	23.52%
28	1512	59.41	27.77	87.18	114.49	27.31	23.85%
29	1513	61.19	31.94	93.13	122.50	29.37	23.98%
30	1514	63.03	36.73	99.76	131.08	31.32	23.90%
31	1515	64.92	42.24	107.16	140.26	33.10	23.60%
32	===						

In the strong example, the Initial Data Area lets you see what's going on. The starting year, the assumptions about the cost structure of the product, and the growth factors are all clearly identified.

Not only can you use the initial mode more quickly, you can modify it faster. (Suppose the user had a different product with an $83 price, a $40 labor cost, and a $10 raw material cost.)

Aristotle once observed "Well begun is half done." The Initial Data Area sketches out the scope of the model before you actually encounter the Model Area. When you have seen the initial values, you can guess at the information to be derived from them. By knowing which terms are the independent assumptions, you have a good idea how the model may be manipulated to achieve a variety of answers.

Storing the data in a separate Initial Data Area makes it easier to ask the "what if" questions that depend on varying the initial data. You can also update a whole set of initial data without getting ensnarled in the thicket of formulas in the Model Area. Keeping the data separate from the model lowers the chance that you will accidentally alter a formula.

Strong

	A B C D E F G H I J K L M N O P Q R
1	ACTIVITY (Activity Tracking) 3 January 1520 T. Tittlemouse
2	26-Apr-89 : Date printed
3	(C) Copyright 1985 by John M. Nevison
4	
5	Track the number of assigned activities during a project.
6	The project is to build a new catapult.
7	
8	To use:
9	1. Enter the new weekly data in the Initial Data.
10	2. Examine the model
11	3. Print the graphs.
12	
13	Contents: (each section is a named range)
14	INTRO . Introduction: Title, description, contents.
15	INITIAL Initial data and beginning assumptions
16	MODEL Quarterly model
17	GRAPH Graphing area
18	VERIFY Verify area
19	--

(continued)

	A	B	C	D	E	F	G	H	I	J	K	L	M	N	O	P	Q	...
20	Initial data and beginning assumptions																	
21		Activities as they occured																
22	Week number	1	2	3	4	5	6	7	8	9	10	11	12	13	14	15	16	...
23	Design activities																	
24	Assigned	5	6	7	7	7	8	7	6	6	5	4	4	3	3	3	2	...
25	Completed	0	3	4	5	6	7	7	6	5	4	5	6	5	4	4	4	...
26	Build activities																	
27	Assigned	0	0	0	0	0	0	3	4	5	4	4	5	6	7	5	6	...
28	Completed	0	0	0	0	0	0	0	2	4	5	4	5	5	6	6	4	...
29	Test activities																	
30	Assigned	0	0	0	0	0	0	0	0	0	0	0	0	0	0	0	0	...
31	Completed	0	0	0	0	0	0	0	0	0	0	0	0	0	0	0	0	...
32	---																	

	A	B	C	D	E	F	...
33	Quarterly model						
34		THE CATAPULT PROJECT: activities completed in early autumn.					
35			1520				
36		Qtr 1	Otr 2	Otr 3	Qtr 4	Total	Date: 3 January 1521
37	Design activities						
38	Assigned Ä	75	11	0	0	86	
39	Completed	63	23	0	0	86	
40	Build activities						
41	Assigned Ä	31	79	14	0	124	
42	Completed	25	71	28	0	124	
43	Test activities Ä Ä						
44	Assigned Ä	0	29	33	1	63	
45	Completed	0	17	35	11	63	
46							
47	Total activities						
48	Assigned	106	119	47	1	273	
49	Completed	88	111	63	11	273	
50	---						

You see again how much easier it is to use a model that extricates the raw numbers from the model itself. ACTIVITY clearly separates raw data from the quarterly model. The user can easily add weekly data without intruding into the Model Area. ACTIVITY labels the initial data so the reader sees that the data are collected weekly to be used in a quarterly fashion. (In fact, data this numerous cry out to be graphed; the full model contains a rather elaborate graphing area to support the spreadsheet's graphs. See Chapter 4 for more details.) A model with unidentified data can turn the reader into a detective.

Weak

	A	B	C	D	E	F	G
1	PLANA	22 Aug 1485	Humpty Dumpty				
2	16-Feb-89	: Date printed					
3							
4	Make a five-year income statement projection.						
5	Begin with sales, subtract costs that are a percentage of sales or are						
6	constant, find net income.						
7							
8	---						
9	Model						
10			1486	1487	1488	1489	1490
11	Sales		100.00	108.00	116.64	125.97	136.05
12	Cost of goods sold		42.50	45.90	49.57	53.54	57.82
13	Gross profit		57.50	62.10	67.07	72.43	78.23
14							
15	S G & A		33.00	35.64	38.49	41.57	44.90
16	Depreciation		7.00	7.00	7.00	7.00	7.00
17	Fixed expenses		40.00	42.64	45.49	48.57	51.90
18							
19	Interest		2.25	2.25	2.25	2.25	2.25
20							
21	Profit before tax		15.25	17.21	19.33	21.61	24.08
22	Tax		6.10	6.88	7.73	8.65	9.63
23	Net Income		9.15	10.33	11.60	12.97	14.45
24							
25	==						

Strong

	A	B	C	D	E	F	G
1	PLANB	22 August 1485	Humpty Dumpty				
2	16-Feb-89	: Date printed					
3							
4	Make a five-year income statement projection.						
5	Begin with sales, subtract costs that are a percentage of sales or are						
6	constant, find net income.						
7							
8	Contents: (each section is a named range)						
9	INTRO	Introduction: Title, description, contents, and map					
10	INITIAL	Initial data and beginning assumptions					
11	MODEL	Income statement projection					
12	---						

(continued)

	A	B	C	D	E	F	G
13	Initial data and beginning assumptions						
14		1486	Starting year				
15		100.00	Sales for starting year				
16		7.00	Depreciation				
17		2.25	Interest				
18	--						
19	Income statement projection						
20			1486	1487	1488	1489	1490
21	Sales		100.00	108.00	116.64	125.97	136.05
22	Cost of goods sold		42.50	45.90	49.57	53.54	57.82
23	Gross profit		57.50	62.10	67.07	72.43	78.23
24							
25	S G & A		33.00	35.64	38.49	41.57	44.90
26	Depreciation		7.00	7.00	7.00	7.00	7.00
27	Fixed expenses		40.00	42.64	45.49	48.57	51.90
28							
29	Interest		2.25	2.25	2.25	2.25	2.25
30							
31	Profit before tax		15.25	17.21	19.33	21.61	24.08
32	Tax		6.10	6.88	7.73	8.65	9.63
33	Net Income		9.15	10.33	11.60	12.97	14.45
34	===						

PLAN B tells you more than PLAN A. You can understand for the first time what the raw data of this model are: the starting year of 1490, the starting sales of $100, the constant $7 depreciation, and the constant $2.25 interest. You feel you have some of the answers to the mystery. Yet for all its improvement over PLAN A, PLAN B is not complete. The witness is still holding back: The spreadsheet still hides assumptions from the reader.

Surface and Label Every Assumption

One of the most serious errors of spreadsheet modeling is burying an assumption. A raw number—a constant, a factor, or a rate—can lurk submerged in a formula in the model. Such an assumption must be forced to the surface and clearly labeled. It should be placed before the model in the Initial Data Area.

Surfacing an assumption gives you an opportunity to label it. This label can go a long way toward explaining the true nature of the model.

Strong

	A	B	C	D	E	F	G
1	PLANC	22 August 1485		Humpty Dumpty			
2	16-Feb-89	: Date printed					
3							
4	Make a five-year income statement projection.						
5	Begin with sales, subtract costs that are a percentage of sales or are						
6	constant, find net income.						
7							
8	Contents: (each section is a named range)						
9	INTRO	Introduction: Title, description, contents, and map					
10	INITIAL	Initial data and beginning assumptions					
11	MODEL	Income statement projection					
12	--						
13	Initial data and beginning assumptions						
14		1486	Starting year				
15		100.00	Sales for starting year				
16		8.0%	Annual sales growth rate				
17		42.5%	Cost of goods sold as a percentage of sales				
18		33.0%	Selling, general, and administrative costs as				
19			a percentage of sales				
20		15.0%	Interest rate				
21		40.0%	Tax rate				
22			1486	1487	1488	1489	1490
23		Depreciation	7.00	7.00	7.00	7.00	7.00
24		Debt	15.00	15.00	15.00	15.00	15.00
25	--						
26	Income statement projection						
27			1486	1487	1488	1489	1490
28	Sales		100.00	108.00	116.64	125.97	136.05
29	Cost of goods sold		42.50	45.90	49.57	53.54	57.82
30	Gross profit		57.50	62.10	67.07	72.43	78.23
31							
32	S G & A		33.00	35.64	38.49	41.57	44.90
33	Depreciation		7.00	7.00	7.00	7.00	7.00
34	Fixed expenses		40.00	42.64	45.49	48.57	51.90
35							
36	Interest		2.25	2.25	2.25	2.25	2.25
37							
38	Profit before tax		15.25	17.21	19.33	21.61	24.08
39	Tax		6.10	6.88	7.73	8.65	9.63
40	Net Income		9.15	10.33	11.60	12.97	14.45
41	==						

Finally you see the hidden detail of PLAN. The buried assumptions are: the 8% annual growth rate, the 42.5% cost of goods sold as a percentage of sales, the 33% selling-general-and-administrative costs as a percentage of sales, the 15% interest rate, and the 40% tax rate. You also see that depreciation and debt are assumed to be constant over the five-year period. Because the constants are spread out in the initial data, the reader may infer that the author thought that it was likely that the user might like to change a value in any year.

Sometimes a spreadsheet identifies the data, but combines the Initial Data Area with another area. This possibility is explored later in this chapter in the section entitled "Common Sense and Spreadsheet Partitioning."

The Model Area

Model to Explain

A model is a web of relations woven with formulas. If you have assiduously separated out raw data and initial assumptions, then the model itself should be pure formulas.

The formulas of the model are themselves assumptions. The first responsibility of the Model Area is to explain clearly what assumptions are embedded in the formulas. The Model Area should provide three levels of explanation:

1. The values that appear in the model.

2. The written explanation of any tricky formulas.

3. The complete printout of all the formulas in the model.

The Model Area's first level of explanation is the values that appear in the cells. If a formula produces results that are not entirely clear, it is a good idea to break the formula into its component pieces, where each step can be viewed.

Weak	*Strong*
1402.08 :Total expense	1402.08 :Total expense
674.08 :Total adjustment	250.00 :Cash advance
	478.00 :Other prepaid
	674.08 :Total adjustment

Here you see how the total travel expenses were reduced by cash advances and prepaid charges (such as conference registrations) to arrive at the total adjustment. In the weak example the intermediate numbers are hidden in a formula; in the strong they are presented as intermediate results.

How much to explain depends on the reader's and the user's backgrounds. When you are in doubt, err on the side of overexplaining. Six months later, oversimplified steps will be a welcome relief as you struggle to read your own model. If someone else uses the model, the steps will increase his or her confidence in its accuracy.

A formula should be easy to read aloud. If a formula gets so complicated that it is hard to read aloud, it probably should be broken into two formulas. If you break a formula into pieces and the intermediate values in the extra cells intrude on the layout of the report you were preparing, create a separate region below the model for making the report.

The Model Area's second level of explanation is a written summary of a tricky formula. The next model changes the independent variable from sales to net income. As a result, the Model Area must explain some tricky formulas.

Strong

	A	B	C	D	E	F	G
1	PLAND	22 February 1486	Tom Tucker				
2	From an original model done 22 August 1485 by Humpty Dumpty						
3	16-Feb-89 : Date printed						
4							
5	Make a five-year income statement projection based on net income growth.						
6	Begin with net income, add costs that are a percentage of net income or						
7	are constant, find sales.						
8							
9	Contents: (each section is a named range)						
10	INTRO	Introduction: Title, description, contents, and map					
11	INITIAL	Initial data and beginning assumptions					
12	MODEL	Income statement projection					
13	--						

(continued)

	A	B	C	D	E	F	G
14	Initial data and beginning assumptions						
15		1486	Starting year				
16		9.15	Net income starting year				
17		10.0%	Annual net income growth rate				
18		464.5%	Cost of goods sold as a percentage of net income				
19		360.7%	Selling, general, and administrative costs as				
20			a percentage of net income				
21		15.0%	Interest rate				
22		40.0%	Tax rate				
23			1486	1487	1488	1489	1490
24	Depreciation		7.00	7.00	7.00	7.00	7.00
25	Debt		15.00	15.00	15.00	15.00	15.00
26	--						
27	Income statement projection						
28							
29	Tricky formulas below include:						
30		Tax from net = (net/(1-tax rate))*tax rate					
31		SG&A = (SG&A %)*Net					
32		Cost of goods sold = (COGS %)*net					
33							
34			1486	1487	1488	1489	1490
35							
36	Net Income		9.15	10.07	11.07	12.18	13.40
37	Tax		6.10	6.71	7.38	8.12	8.93
38	Profit before tax		15.25	16.78	18.45	20.30	22.33
39							
40	Interest		2.25	2.25	2.25	2.25	2.25
41	S G & A		33.00	36.30	39.93	43.92	48.32
42	Depreciation		15.00	15.00	15.00	15.00	15.00
43	Fixed expenses		48.00	51.30	54.93	58.92	63.32
44							
45	Cost of goods sold		42.50	46.75	51.43	56.57	62.22
46	Gross profit		33.00	36.30	39.93	43.92	48.32
47	Sales		75.50	83.05	91.36	100.49	110.54
48	===						

You need help with the formulas in this model because PLAN D turns PLAN C on its head. PLAN C began with sales and ended with net income; PLAN D does the reverse. In the inverted model, a few formulas get tricky; they have been explained near where they occur. PLAN D also reverses the order of the lines in the model to make the top-to-bottom flow of the reader correspond to the top-to-bottom flow of the calculation. The Model Area is trying above all to explain how the calculations are performed. In order to get an easy-to-read report, a Report Area can be added (see Chapter 4 for details).

The Model Area's third level of explanation of the calculations is a printed copy of all the formulas in the model. In the case of PLAN D they might look like this:

First three years of model (detail):

	A B	C	D	E
34		1486	1487	1488
35				
36	Net Income	9.15	10.07	11.07
37	Tax	6.10	6.71	7.38
38	Profit before tax	15.25	16.78	18.45
39				
40	Interest	2.25	2.25	2.25
41	S G & A	33.00	36.30	39.93
42	Depreciation	15.00	15.00	15.00
43	Fixed expenses	48.00	51.30	54.93
44				
45	Cost of goods sold	42.50	46.75	51.43
46	Gross profit	33.00	36.30	39.93
47	Sales	75.50	83.05	91.36

First three years of model as formulas (detail):

	A B	C	D	E
34		+B15	+C34+1	+D34+1
35				
36	Net Income	+$B$16	+C36*(1+$B$17)	+D36*(1+$B$17)
37	Tax	+C36/(1-$B$22)*$B$22	+D36/(1-$B$22)*$B$22	+E36/(1-$B$22)*$B$22
38	Profit before tax	+C36+C37	+D36+D37	+E36+E37
39				
40	Interest	+$B$21*C25	+$B$21*D25	+$B$21*E25
41	S G & A	+$B$19*C36	+$B$19*D36	+$B$19*E36
42	Depreciation	+C25	+D25	+E25
43	Fixed expenses	+C41+C42	+D41+D42	+E41+E42
44				
45	Cost of goods sold	+$B$18*C36	+$B$18*D36	+$B$18*E36
46	Gross profit	+C39+C41+C44	+D39+D41+D44	+E39+E41+E44
47	Sales	+C46+C45	+D46+D45	+E46+E45

Be sure when you print a paper copy of the finished model for the reader that you print a second copy with the model's formulas. (See Chapter 8 for more on this idea.) Details on how to print formulas are in the appendices.

Formulas may well appear in other parts of the spreadsheet besides the Model Area. A frequent use of a formula in the Initial Data Area is to be sure that one piece of data implies another. For example, if you wish to divide something between two players using a percentage, the results might look like this:

Weak	*Strong (formula)*	*Strong (values)*
.14 Player A	.14 Player A	14% Player A
.86 Player B	(1-$A$5) Player B	86% Player B

The strong version uses a formula to avoid an entry error. One entry gets two correct results.

Formulas may occur in other regions as well. Wherever a formula appears, its function should be apparent and in support of the particular area's purpose (see Chapter 4 for more on other areas).

Point to the Right Source

As you build your formulas, you will have occasion to refer to an earlier cell for a value. Whenever you do this, be sure you are referring to the right occurrence of the value. That is, be sure you point to the value that makes it easiest for the reader and user to understand the formula.

If the best source is another cell in the body of the model, it will be nearby and will have the context of the model to help explain it. If the best source is in the initial data, it will probably have some explanatory text near it. The right source is the one that speeds the reader's comprehension of the formula.

For example, consider the following three lines from the body of the model in Plan C.

Strong

	A	B	C	D
32	S G & A		+$B$18*C28	+$B$18*D28
33	Depreciation		+C23	+D23
34	Fixed expenses		+C32+C33	+D32+D33

The formula for selling, general, and administrative costs (S G & A) uses the fixed percentage found in the initial area at $B$17. Initial data items that appear as single values are often used as "absolute" cells in model formulas. In this case, pointing to the original source is the method that best illustrates what the formula means.

In line 33, however, you see a different solution to the problem. The good formula C33=+C31+C32 says "add the two lines above." Fixed expenses equals S G &A plus depreciation. Any other form would make more work for the reader. The poor alternative C33=+C31+C22 embroils the reader in an unnecessary search for the what's going on up in row 22.

When a line, a column, or a row of initial data such as Depreciation is repeated in the model itself, the best course is usually to refer to the nearby line in the model. The nearby line is easier to find.

An isolated single value, however, is almost always better referred to the original source. If you make it a habit to refer to the original source, the reader of the paper version can make sense out of the model more quickly, and the user of the model can handle the model with greater certainty. Both people know that if they change the model in the Initial Data Area they are changing the unique reference point that feeds formulas all over the model.

The Dual Role of the Model Area

In the basic form, the Model Area plays two roles—as the area that explains the calculations and as the area that displays the results. Because many spreadsheets can be built with the Model Area also serving the purpose of the Report Area, the discussion of the Report Area is deferred to Chapter 4. If a conflict arises between being clear about the calculation and displaying the results, a Report Area should be added.

The basic form is the essential first step of good spreadsheet design. The Introduction, the Initial Data Area, and the Model Area form a powerful triumvirate, the fundamental triad of a good design. The 10 basic rules in this chapter will help you build models that can be used and reused with confidence.

Using the Basic Form

Even with the Report Area discussion deferred, serious questions remain about the relationship between the Initial Data Area and the Model Area. At first, the idea of a separate Initial Data Area may appear to violate the fundamental simplicity of spreadsheets. But remember that the rule is not "Set up an Initial Data Area," the rule is "Identify the data."

The mystery spreadsheet below focuses the issue. What do you call it?

Mystery spreadsheet

	Column of row sums
Mass of raw	.
numbers in	.
a large table.	.
Row of column sums…	Grand total

Is this an Initial Data Area with a few extra formulas? A Model Area without an Initial Data Area? Or a Report Area without an Initial Data Area or a Model Area?

To answer these questions remind yourself that the Initial Data Area identifies the raw data, the Model Area explains the calculation and the Report Area prints the results for a particular reader. If you can make one area display the raw data, explain the calculation, and print out clear results, then call it an Initial Data Area. The first requirement is the greatest requirement: You must always identify the data.

If the mystery spreadsheet is an Initial Data Area with a few added formulas, and if you add more formulas to the first few, at what point should the spreadsheet spawn a Model Area?

First form

Initial Data Area

	Column of row sums
Mass of raw	.
INTERMEDIATE ROW OF FORMULAS	.
numbers in	.
INTERMEDIATE ROW OF FORMULAS	.
a large table.	.
Row of column sums…	Grand total

When should you split this into two areas? When you become uncomfort-able thinking that identifying the data is the primary purpose of the spread-sheet. When the calculations become confused or obscure. When you need room to rearrange the model to make it easier to read. Any one of these rea-sons is sufficient cause for a Model Area.

Second form

Initial Data Area

Mass of raw
        numbers in
                a large table
                        (with explanations.)

Model Area

                                        Column of row sums
Mass of raw   .
INTERMEDIATE ROW OF FORMULAS   .
        numbers in   .
INTERMEDIATE ROW OF FORMULAS   .
                a large table.   .

Row of column sums...   Grand total

When you break the spreadsheet into two areas you may be bothered by seeing a big block of numbers twice, but you will find compensatory free-doms. You will be able to label the Initial Data clearly without intruding on your model's format. You will also be able to shape the model to reveal what the calculations are and to convince the reader that these calculations are correct.

If separating the Initial Data Area and the Model Area makes you feel stupid at first, do it anyway. If, after a few months of going out of your way to apply these rules, your models are not substantially better, back off from this practice until you find a balance that is right for you and for the users of your spreadsheets. Your overriding concern should be for ease of use over ease of construction, for clarity of expression over speed of writing.

A Word on Building the Initial Data Area and the Model Area

When writing a new model, one way to develop the initial data is by beginning with a template like NEW and building the Model Area first. When you write a formula with a constant in it (for example, King Henry's 23 percent tax rate in Chapter 1), you can stop, write, and label the assumption up in the Initial Data Area, return to the model, and rewrite the formula with a reference to the Initial Data Area.

So the old formula may have looked like this:

B30 = +A30*.23

and the new formula looks like this:

B30 = +A30*$B$5

and B5 and B6 look like this:

23% tax rate

As you continue building the model you may find a row or column of raw numbers. Again you move the raw numbers up to the Initial Data Area and change the model entry to a one-term formula that refers to the raw data.

So you will have changed the old model:

B36 = 18,346

to the new model:

B36 = +B15

where the new initial data is:

B15 = 18,346.

The result of these efforts will be a Model Area that is entirely formulas. Such efforts will force you to think about the spreadsheet's use while the spreadsheet model is being built. The final spreadsheet will benefit from this extra thought.

Spreadsheets That Do Not Have Model Areas

Some spreadsheets are exceptions to the basic rules. Rules should aid your common sense, not replace it. Some spreadsheets honestly do not need a Model Area. Here's one example:

Strong

	A	B	C	D	E	F	G	H	I
1	TRAVEL 15 June 1588 Queen Elizabeth								
2									
3	Print the Queen's travel expenses.								
4	To use:								
5	1. Call up program and save with a new name.								
6	2. Enter trip information in the appropriate places.								
7	3. Collect all the prepaid expenses as a formula in the "prepaid expenses" cell.								
8	4. Include appropriate notes.								
9	5. Print a copy for your personal records and a copy for the Treasury.								
10									
11	--								
12	Initial data, beginning assumptions, and travel report.								
13		TRAVEL EXPENSES OF QUEEN ELIZABETH							
14									
15	Date: 23-28 September 1588			Purpose: To talk with the lords and visit					
16	Name: Queen Elizabeth			the people.					
17	Trip: Visit to Banbury Cross								
18									
19		SUN	MON	TUE	WED	THR	FRI	SAT	TOTAL
20	Travel		96.00	96.00	110.00	80.00	96.00		478.00
21	Local trans								0.00
22	Stable		24.00	32.00	38.00	44.00	23.00		161.00
23	Inn	104.85	97.97	103.77	100.42	95.57			502.58
24	Meals								0.00
25	Breakfast		8.00	8.00		35.00	5.00		56.00
26	Lunch			5.00		5.00	45.00		55.00
27	Dinner	15.50	25.00	45.00	27.00		10.00		122.50
28	Entertainment		3.00	4.00	2.00	4.00	3.00		16.00
29	Miscellaneous		3.00		8.00				11.00
30									
31	Total	120.35	256.97	293.77	285.42	263.57	182.00	0.00	1,402.08
32									
33	1402.08 :Total expense Signed: ______________________________________								
34	250.00 :Treasury advance								
35	478.00 :Other (prepaid) Date: ____________								
36	674.08 :Total adjustment								
37									
38	0.00 :Due treasury								
39	674.08 :Due Queen								
40									
41									
42	Notes: Tue. dinner with Mayor.								
43	Thursday b'fast with castle force,								
44	Fri. lunch with General.								
45									
46	==								

TRAVEL is a spreadsheet that does not need a Model Area. It has only a very few simple equations. Its purpose is to identify the initial data and present it clearly, so the author calls it an Initial Data Area with a few totals. We do not have a Model Area at all. What we print out is the Initial Data Area.

Databases are another case where the Initial Data Area overwhelms the Model Area. Often, however, databases trail summary reports that are Model Areas.

Strong

	A	B	C	D	E	F
1	SHEEP 15 April 1566 Bo Peep					
2	16-Feb-89 : Date printed					
3						
4	Maintain a database on the sheep herd. Track the number and value					
5	of the lost and found sheep. Revise it periodically to keep it current.					
6						
7	WARNING: This model will be incorrect between the time the data is					
8	resorted and the model's functions are revised. (See directions for details.)					
9						
10	Contents: (each section is a named range)					
11	INTRO Introduction: Title, description, contents, and directions					
12	INITIAL Initial data and beginning assumptions					
13	MODEL Sheep count model					
14	GRAPH Sheep pie chart data					
15						
16	Directions:					
17						
18	1. Correct the "lost" and "found" status of the sheep in the initial data.					
19	2. Sort the initial data to group all the lost sheep together.					
20	3. Revise the COUNT functions under "Number" in the model to count					
21	the two groups of lost and found.					
22	4. Revise the SUM functions under "Value" in the model to sum					
23	the value of the two groups of lost and found					
24	5. Call up pie chart entitled SHEEP'S PIE.					
25	--					

(continued)

	A	B	C	D	E	F
26	Initial data and beginning assumptions					
27						
28	NAME	STATUS	COLOR	VALUE		
29	Brian	Found	White	100		
30	Ian	Found	White	200		
31	Margaret	Found	Plaid	200		
32	Angus	Found	Black	300		
33	Janet	Lost	White	400		
34	Hugh	Lost	Red	300		
35	Alistair	Lost	White	100		
36	Mary	Lost	White	100		
37	Agnus	Lost	White	200		
38	---					
39	Sheep count model					
40		Number	Percent	Value		
41	Lost	5	56%	1100		
42	Found	4	44%	800		
43	Total	9	100%	1900		
44						
45	---					
46	Sheep pie chart data					
47			Value	Percent value		
48		Lost	1100	58%		
49		Found	800	42%		
50	===					

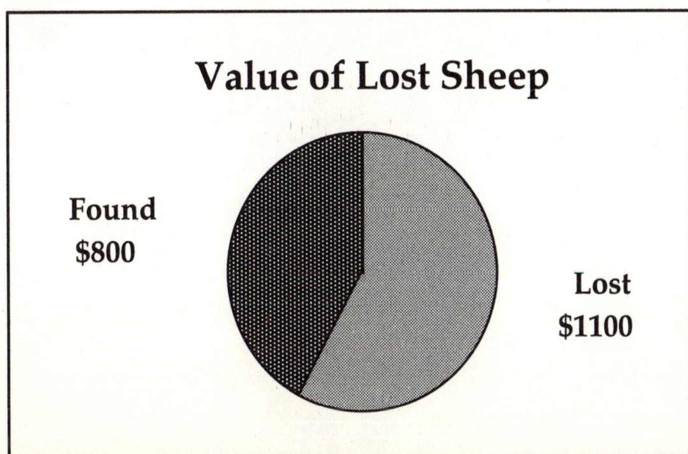

Figure 2–1. Bo Peep's Pie Chart.

Sheep is a collection of data with a modest model wagging along behind. There are no major assumptions, just a collection of data. Notice that the model has spun off a graphics area (more on that in Chapter 4). A major reason for dividing a spreadsheet into areas is that it makes later modification easier.

With a very large database you might want to rearrange the contents to have two different areas for data: an area for the "what if" initial assumptions, and a database for the bulk of the raw data.

Data in a database may be so large and changing that you want to keep it below the rest of the model. This practice has the advantage that the location of your reports remains stable because it is above the insertion and deletion of rows that constantly vary the size of the database. If the sheep herd had numbered in the hundreds, Bo Peep might have structured the model like this:

Strong

	A	B	C	D	E	F
5	Contents: (each section is a named range)					
6	INTRO	Introduction: Title, description, contents, and directions				
7	INITIAL	Initial data and beginning assumptions				
8	MODEL	Sheep count model				
9	GRAPH	Sheep pie chart data				
10	DATA	Database of sheep data				

3

The Mind's Eye: Design

MULTIPLICATION IS VEXATION
Multiplication is vexation,
    Division is as bad;
The Rule of Three doth puzzle me,
    And Practice drives me mad.

The problem of design is one of working out ideas in advance and of testing completed structures. Design also encompasses an abiding concern for the overall appearance of things. The next four procedural rules help you apply the first 10. They suggest what to do and when: They are rules for the mind's eye.

First Design on Paper

Do your first thinking with pencil and paper. Design can encompass many things, but one thing is certain: Your first idea will not be your last and only rarely will it be your best. Ideas demand editing. You will need to react to your initial impulse, to brood over your vision, to rearrange, to revise, to rethink. All of this is much easier done on paper. If you resist the intemperate urge to type on the computer and instead deliberate over your initial design on paper, you will complete your whole project faster.

If you cannot resist the urge to leap to your computer and begin typing, please think of your first efforts as being "paper" efforts. Use nonsense collections of letters such as "xxx yyy xxx" to simulate text, and rows or columns of 99999.99 to simulate quickly what a block of numbers will look like. Move blocks of your spreadsheets around until you have a good feel for the gross arrangement of the whole model. In short, tell yourself that your first efforts are to sketch a preliminary design and to mull over basic ideas.

When beginning an absolutely new model, some find it helpful to write a one-sentence statement of purpose that begins "The purpose of this spreadsheet is … " This sentence can be followed by a paragraph that begins, "How the spreadsheet achieves this purpose is … " For people who think best with words, these two phrases can cut a clear path through a lot of fuzzy thinking.

For those who prefer pictures, sketches on a large piece of paper can be a big help. You can lay out each region as a block. Within a region, columns and rows can appear as subblocks. Areas for text can be outlined to see how the general shape and size will appear. The blocks can be arranged so that they relate to each other in the best way. Blocks that create information can be placed ahead of blocks that use the information.

Your model will be easier to read if you group areas that work together. A tricky formula is easier to explore if its constituent elements lie nearby. Grouping allows nearby references to be quickly checked.

Design from the major idea to the minor. Start with the area of central importance—the model, or the database—and work out to the minor regions—back to the initial data and description, forward to submodels that compute pieces of data, over to collateral models that develop parallel figures. Sometimes the area of central importance will be a report, sometimes a graph.

Don't be surprised if the region of central importance shifts. Sometimes you may begin thinking your model's report is the central idea, only to discover that the real heart of the matter is a graph. Stay clear in your own mind about what the major idea is. This clarity of purpose will allow you to design faster and better.

If your current idea is not a totally new idea, sometimes an old design can serve as a template for your new project. By using a template you are less likely to overlook a necessary part and more likely to cast your final ideas in a form familiar to your eye. Be sure that you don't let the old idea unnecessarily restrict you. Be prepared to break the mold and move on to a new and better approach if your idea requires it.

If you have been doing your initial "paper" design on the computer, remember that you can systematically extract regions from the rough draft and move them to a brand new spreadsheet (or insert them into a preexisting template). Extracting a few good regions is sometimes faster than editing many bad regions. When you extract, you will lose special definitions of column width and special formats for cells.

Design your spreadsheet once so that it can be used many times. One hard test for a good design is ease of reuse. If a model is easy to reuse, it is probably designed in a straightforward manner. If you think about how the model could be used a year from now, you will probably design it better. Design it to last five years.

Test and Edit

A correct model requires practice just as clear English requires proofreading. As you work on your model in solitude, do both. You can practice your spreadsheet by varying the initial parameters and seeing if the appropriate conclusions are altered in the expected way. You can proofread your comments by being sure they stay current with the model as you build and revise it.

You may more fully test a model by using a known example to be sure the answer agrees with the known correct answer. You may use 0s and 1s for a quick practice, but you should avoid them when providing sample data to verify formally that the final model is correct.

Weak

	A	B	C	D	E	F	G	H
43	Model							
44	Tricky formulas:							
45	Expected = (low + 4*likely + high)/6							
46	Standard deviation = (high − low)/6							
47	Variance = (standard deviation)^2							
48	Project standard deviation = square root(project variance)							
49								
50	Task name		Low	Likely	High	Expected	Variance	
51	Activity 1		0	3	6	3.0	1.0	
52	Activity 2		0	3	6	3.0	1.0	
53	Activity 3		0	3	6	3.0	1.0	
54	Activity 4		0	3	6	3.0	1.0	
55	Activity 5		0	3	6	3.0	1.0	
56	Activity 6		0	3	6	3.0	1.0	
57	Activity 7		0	3	6	3.0	1.0	
58	Activity 8		0	3	6	3.0	1.0	
59	Activity 9		0	3	6	3.0	1.0	
60								Standard deviation
61	Project totals					27.0	9.0	3.0
62	Check sums		0	27	54	27.0		
63	---							

Strong

	A	B	C	D	E	F	G	H
43	Model							
44	Tricky formulas:							
45	Expected = (low + 4*likely + high)/6							
46	Standard deviation = (high – low)/6							
47	Variance = (standard deviation)^2							
48	Project standard deviation = square root(project variance)							
49								
50	Task name	Low	Likely	High	Expected	Variance		
51	Activity 1	2	5	14	6.0	4.0		
52	Activity 2	2	5	14	6.0	4.0		
53	Activity 3	2	5	14	6.0	4.0		
54	Activity 4	2	5	14	6.0	4.0		
55	Activity 5	2	5	14	6.0	4.0		
56	Activity 6	2	5	14	6.0	4.0		
57	Activity 7	2	5	14	6.0	4.0		
58	Activity 8	2	5	14	6.0	4.0		
59	Activity 9	2	5	14	6.0	4.0		
60							Standard deviation	
61	Project totals				54.0	36.0	6.0	
62	Check sums	18	45	126	54.0			
63	--							

The test data should try to avoid 0s and 1s because they do special things that might mask errors. For example, 1^2 is 1 while 2^2 is 4. If there were a mistake in squaring the standard deviation to compute the variance, it would not be visible if the standard deviation was 1. In test data, use numbers that change things. A number added to 0 or multiplied by 1, does not.

A strong set of test data can be checked by hand. This model has four tricky equations that can be verified by inspection when a strong set of initial data is applied. The numbers 2 and 14 are the smallest positive whole numbers (larger than one) that yield a standard deviation that is a whole number bigger than 1. Five is the smallest whole number between 2 and 14 that yields a whole number for the expected value. Nine is the smallest number of tasks that yields a project standard deviation different from the task standard deviation.

If you write your introduction as you write your model, you will have an extra check on your thinking and you will be able to start your proofreading early. As you continue your work, you should pause and proofread. Rewrite your words when they need it—don't put off the rewriting until the last minute.

Never release a spreadsheet for use until you have read the whole thing on paper. Paper is quiet. Paper is large. Paper allows your eye to range over the entirety of the model. Paper gives your common sense a chance to engage the model's results in a dialogue.

After you feel you have completed your model, allow someone else to exercise it and to proofread it. Listen to his or her responses and revise your work accordingly. Your final model will be better for it.

Keep it Visible

A finished model must be written for the reader of the printed version. The decision to use the model is often based on the printed version, so it is critically important that the model make all the facts available to the reader. The model must keep the information visible.

Spreadsheets allow a number of things to be hidden. Formulas and formats lurk behind numbers. Constants can hide in formulas. Named ranges can lie waiting in the framework and never be explained. Graphs can hang on models and not be revealed to the reader. For the on-line user of a simple spreadsheet, these hidden concerns may be only an annoyance. But for the off-line reader of a completed model all these concerns matter a great deal.

As you work on your model, ask yourself "How will the reader (not the user) know this?" Answer the question by making the idea visible. Tricky formulas can be explained. Unusual formats can be described. Some named ranges can be included in the table of contents, others can be collected in an alphabetical index. Graphs can be listed at the beginning of the graphing section.

If you seriously try to create a model whose printed version you can read and understand, you will succeed in keeping your ideas visible. A great many models fail because their authors wrote for the user of the model and not for the reader of the model. The user is important and you are not forgetting him or her when you write for the reader. In fact, quite the contrary: If you write for the reader, you will help the user as well. The user is also a reader and any time saved by reading the facts rather than discovering them embedded in the model will speed the model's productive use.

Space So the Spreadsheet May be Easily Read

Smooth the path for the reader's eye. Make it easy for him or her to peruse your model. Space paragraphs. Wherever possible, use space between rows or columns rather than lines. Use initial capital letters followed by lowercase letters in most titles. When you use lines or double lines to separate items, make the ink a symbol of something important: The models in this book use a single line to border the bottom of an area, and a double line to border the bottom of a submodel.

Strong

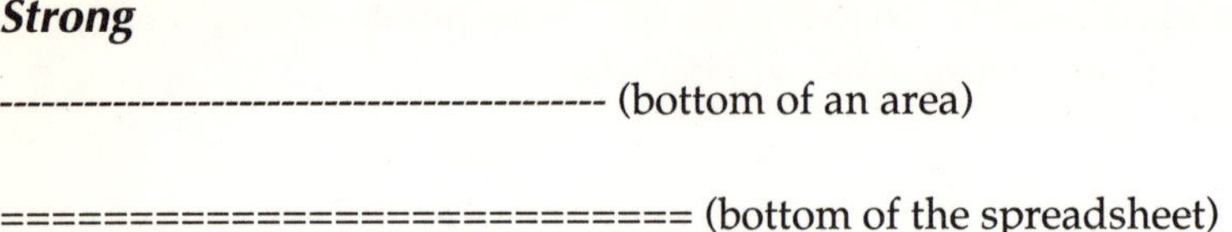

In general, keep models to the left side of the page where the reader expects to begin a new area or a new paragraph. Most of the models in this book are arranged vertically so that the next section of a model appears below the current one. This vertical arrangement makes it easier to conclude a paragraph with a blank line, and an area with a dashed line.

A note of caution about spacing: Spacing within the body of a block of numbers in the model area should be included **late** in the model's development. When you revise a model and try to copy a formula down an interrupted column or try to connect a graphing area to a model with an interrupted row you will notice the inconvenience of the inserted spaces.

If you do insert spaces into the body of a block of numbers—say at every fifth line to make the numbers easier to read—do it just before you put the model to bed.

Weak (easy to work with)	*Strong (easy to read)*
123 456 789 111 222	123 456 789 111 222
987 654 321 999 333	987 654 321 999 333
888 777 666 999 444	888 777 666 999 444
222 444 666 888 111	222 444 666 888 111
432 543 654 765 876	432 543 654 765 876
123 345 234 234 543	
765 345 987 234 765	123 345 234 234 543
234 123 544 235 654	765 345 987 234 765
123 456 123 554 342	234 123 544 235 654
453 765 675 876 786	123 456 123 554 342
987 786 654 543 432	453 765 675 876 786
234 432 543 666 777	
888 999	987 786 654 543 432
	234 432 543 666 777
	888 999

The inserted lines literally give the eye a much needed break. The lines also allow the reader to count the data quickly. The strong example reveals that the numbers are arrayed in 13 lines.

When you wake the model up for a different day's work:

1. Remove the blank lines to reestablish the contiguous blocks of numbers.

2. Do your work—inserting new rows, deleting old columns, and copying formulas across and down.

3. Reinsert blank lines at the end of the session.

Your Own Reader

More than all but the most hardened user, you will be the reader of your own spreadsheets. If you begin with a careful design and test your results, if you keep your ideas visible and are kind to the reader's eye, you will greatly speed your own work. This speed is the consequence of being kind to yourself, to your own mind's eye.

4

Other Functions, Other Forms

The basic three-part spreadsheet—Introduction, Initial Data Area, and Model Area—can only go so far. As you work with spreadsheets, a variety of quite complex tasks will require different actions and additional areas on your spreadsheets. You will need other forms for other functions.

Give a New Function a New Area

The esthetic of larger spreadsheets is that distinct activities deserve distinct areas on the spreadsheet. This does not always happen because some people do not know how to keep a large number of regions under control with a table of contents and a map. Others think it is too much extra work to put into a "simple" spreadsheet. Most still do not understand how important it is to make a model easy to modify later.

As soon as someone suggests that a model should be easy to modify, giving a new function a new area becomes a reasonable idea. If modification means a change in some function, then the part to change is easy to locate: It is the area where the current function is done. When you want to alter a report you go to the report area. When you wish to change a graph you modify the graph and perhaps the graphing area in the spreadsheet. When you want to alter a macro, you go to the macro area. Giving a new function a new area is a simple way to let form follow function.

When this idea was applied to computer programs in the early 1970s, experience showed that the programs could be modified in half the time. Because modifying programs accounted for 80 percent of the cost of programming, cutting this cost in half represented an overall saving of 40 percent of the effort in working with a computer program! Applying this lesson to your spreadsheets will save you a great deal of time and effort.

This table of contents from a project management spreadsheet shows how powerful this idea can be in practice.

Strong

Contents:

Introduction   Input Area
Initial Data Area
Report Area
   Report on budgeted project by task
   Report on budgeted project by week
   Report on budgeted project by worker
   Report on actual project to date by task
   Report on actual project to date by week
   Report on actual project to date by worker
   Report of budget versus actual, by week, worker, and task
Graph Area
   Project budgeted versus actual
   Bar chart of workers actual
Macro Area
   Queries on the database
   Choosing a report to print
Project Database

You can see from the contents alone where new functions grow in new areas. These areas address two kinds of functions. First, the generic behavior of the spreadsheet leads to areas such as database, graphics, and macros. Second, within these areas the requirements of business require special places for a particular report or a special graph. The table of contents shows that the project database is at the bottom of the spreadsheet. The information in the database is collected in a series of reports. The Graph Area collects those items that need to be graphed. The Macro Area contains those macros necessary to smooth the work of the program.

If someone needs a different report on workers and their actual accomplishments, you know right where to go to begin your work: the "Report on actual project to date by worker." (If the Report Area fully documents its ties to other areas, you will also know if you must explore the Graph Area and the Macro Area for related details.)

If the need arises to revise one of the charts or graphs that this spreadsheet produces, you will know to look in the Graph Area. If a new week's data arrives you know where to go to enter it in the database. Because the spreadsheet grew new business functions (the reports) in new areas, when the business need changes the spreadsheet will change in the appropriate area.

A final note on major and minor function. The dominating assumption in the foregoing discussion is that the whole spreadsheet was devoted to one major business function. If, in the course of combining activities in one physical spreadsheet, you find two or more distinct business functions, subordinate spreadsheet function to business function.

Weak	*Strong*
Introduction	Introduction
Verify Area	Verify Area
Initial Data Area	Submodel for business function 1
Data for business function 1	Initial data
Data for business function 2	Model area
Model Area	Report A
Model of business function 1	Graphing area
Model of business function 2	Chart A
Report Area	Chart B
Report A on business function 1	Macro A
Report B on business function 2	
Report C on business function 2	Submodel for business function 2
Graph Area	Initial Data Area
Chart A on business function 1	Model Area
Chart B on business function 1	Report Area
Chart C on business function 2	Report B
Chart D on business function 2	Report C
Macro Area	Graph Area
Macro A on business function 1	Chart C
Macro B on business function 2	Chart D
	Macro B

Business function is more important than spreadsheet function because changes in business function drive changes in your spreadsheets. (Only rarely will changes in spreadsheets drive changes in business.) To modify a spreadsheet quickly, it should be organized to respond to changes in business function.

Remember that Lotus 1-2-3 Release 3 includes pages of spreadsheets where each page has an upper-left corner labeled A1, for example, A:A1, B:A1, and C:A1. You may use these pages to give a new function not just a new area, but a new page. In 1-2-3 Release 3 the last example might look like this:

Strong	*Strong in Release 3*	
Introduction	+A:A1	Introduction
Verify Area	+A:A1	Verify Area
Submodel for business function 1	+B:A1	Submodel for business function 1
Initial Data Area	+B:A1	Initial Data Area
Model Area	+B:A1	Model Area
Report A	+C:A1	Report A
Graphing Area	+D:A1	Graphing Area
Chart A	+D:A1	Chart A
Chart B	+D:A1	Chart B
Macro A	+E: A1	Macro A
Submodel for business function 2	+F:A1	Submodel for business function 2
Initial Data Area	+F:A1	Initial Data Area
Model Area	+F:A1	Model Area
Report Area	+G:A1	Report Area
Report B	+G:A1	Report B
Report C	+H:A1	Report C
Graphing Area	+I:A1	Graphing Area
Chart C	+I:A1	Chart C
Chart D	+I:A1	Chart D
Macro B	+J:A1	Macro B

A new page can appear with a new submodel, a new Report Area, a new Graph Area, or a new set of macros. In the strong example, the dynamic table of contents (see "Map the Contents" in Chapter 2 for additional details) ensures that when you later insert or delete a page, the references will adjust automatically and continue to point to the correct section.

Report to Your Reader

The purpose of a report is to communicate as clearly and concisely as possible with a particular reader. Think about your reader as you fashion the report. If he or she is interested in your report, you may put the important points last; if not, put them first. If a reader likes to know when the report was made, include the date and time. If the reader is already familiar with a certain style, or layout, present the information in that style. Remember that if the reader does not read the report, he or she won't receive the information you wish to convey. Your report should arrest the eye, engage the attention, and win the conviction of your reader.

If you allow yourself a region for each report, you will give yourself the elbow room you need to fashion crisp, appropriate, compelling reports. If you try to format one basic model to please all your readers you may end up pleasing none.

What you say and how you say it will vary with whom you wish to say it to. Nevertheless, here is a short list to help you remember some essentials.

1. Lay it out in a familiar style: Conform to department practices.

2. Lay it out in an appealing style.

3. Use typographic variation for emphasis.

4. Include the name of the company and the work group within the company where appropriate.

5. Give a full, accurate title.

6. Include the date and, usually, the time.

7. Introduce the report in plain English.

8. Reference related graphs, macros, and models when appropriate.

9. Include information on how to contact the author, when appropriate.

10. Group numbers that must be compared.

11. Abbreviate numbers to their useful level of significance.

12. Go from row causes to column effects.

13. Work from left to right—the way the reader reads.

14. Have the reader proofread the report for content and format before it becomes official.

Strong

	A	B	C	D	E	F	G	H
1	12-Jun-60		OUR DEPARTMENT'S QUARTERLY PERFORMANCE					
2			FOR MONTH OF MAY (Month 2 of Quarter 2)					
3		Quarter to date				Until end of quarter		
4		Plan	Actual	Rate		Plan	To go	Rate
5	Sales	58	54.0	93%		79.0	25.0	68%
6	Costs	40.6	39.5	97%		57.8	18.3	68%
7	Profits	17.4	14.5	83%		21.2	6.7	68%
8								
9	We are close to being on target. Let's keep up the good work!							
10	The third month will be a big one. We can make our sales target if we							
11	continue at the level of the last two months. Let's go for it!							
12	---							

Here's a straightforward report. It is laid out in the style familiar to the department for which it was written. It uses capital and lowercase letters to emphasize the title. In real life it would contain the name of the actual department where it says "OUR DEPARTMENT" now. It has a full accurate title and it contains the date it was printed. It contains a few words of interpretation and encouragement. The numbers that are being compared are close together and clearly labeled. The numbers have been abbreviated to their useful level of significance. The same basic report might appear in different wrapping in different departments. Here are two alternatives:

Strong

	A	B	C	D	E	F	G	H
13	NURSERY KINGDOM	*** CONFIDENTIAL INFORMATION ***						
14								
15	Spreadsheet name: DEPT-BUDG							
16	Last revised: 3 June 1560							
17	Last revised by: M. Contrary							
18	Date: 12 June 1560							
19	Division: Outdoor							
20	Dept: Garden							
21								

(continued)

	A	B	C	D	E	F	G	H
22			GARDEN DEPARTMENT'S QUARTERLY PERFORMANCE					
23			FOR MONTH OF MAY (Month 2 of Quarter 2)					
24			Quarter to date			Until end of quarter		
25			Plan	Actual	Rate	Plan	To go	Rate
26	Sales		58	54.0	93%	79.0	25.0	68%
27	Costs		40.6	39.5	97%	57.8	18.3	68%
28	Profits		17.4	14.5	83%	21.2	6.7	68%
29								

The first of these alternatives has a definite form that identifies the company, division, department, who is currently responsible for the results, and when the relevant work was performed.

Strong

	A	B	C	D	E	F	G	H
30	Outdoor division, Garden Department					NURSERY KINGDOM		
31								
32	Printed on: 12 June 1560				DEPT-BUDG	:Source spreadsheet		
33					M. Contrary	:Last modified by		
34					OG5-375566.1	:Document number		
35					Unclassified	:Classification		
36								
37			GARDEN DEPARTMENT'S QUARTERLY PERFORMANCE					
38			FOR MONTH OF MAY (Month 2 of Quarter 2)					
39			Quarter to date			Until end of quarter		
40			Plan	Actual	Rate	Plan	To go	Rate
41	Sales		58	54.0	93%	79.0	25.0	68%
42	Costs		40.6	39.5	97%	57.8	18.3	68%
43	Profits		17.4	14.5	83%	21.2	6.7	68%
44								

The second alternative is a form that might be familiar to the reader employed by a federal, state, or local government. Note that this version includes a document number, and an explicit location for the classification of the document (unclassified, classified, secret, etc.).

When you do two-dimensional tables, remember that a person reads from row causes to column results. Consider the following table and two possible reports.

Weak

	A	B	C	D	E	F	G
23	Model						
24	Observed cell counts						
25			Elves	Fairies	Goblins	Trolls	Total
26		Unicorns	9	7	2	0	18
27		Griffins	3	6	9	2	20
28		Dragons	1	2	5	8	16
29							
30		Total	13	15	16	10	54

The model itself betrays a prejudice that mythical beasts pick their mythical masters. When the report from this model is prepared it could look like this:

Strong

	A	B	C	D	E	F	G
10	18-Nov-90						
11		PETS CHOOSE THEIR MASTERS					
12			Elves	Fairies	Goblins	Trolls	Total
13		Unicorns	50%	39%	11%	0%	100%
14		Griffins	15%	30%	45%	10%	100%
15		Dragons	6%	13%	31%	50%	100%
16							

Notice that the title of the report asserts the row cause affects the column results, "Pets choose their masters." The percentages are across the page so that the reader can compare the actors, the pets.

The initial information allows an alternative interpretation. Masters could choose their pets. You could assert this by arranging the same data in a different way.

Strong

	A	B	C	D	E	F
17	18-Nov-90					
18		MASTERS CHOOSE THEIR PETS				
19			Unicorns	Griffins	Dragons	Total
20		Elves	69%	23%	8%	100%
21		Fairies	47%	40%	13%	100%
22		Goblins	13%	56%	31%	100%
23		Trolls	0%	20%	80%	100%
24						

Here the reverse assertion is made in the title and supported by the row-cause, column-effect arrangement of the report. Again, the percentages across make it easy to compare between the actors. Here it is clear that elves greatly prefer unicorns, trolls greatly prefer dragons, fairies are more evenly divided, and goblins have a slight preference for griffins. If you wanted to compare effects, you would run percentages down the columns.

Sometimes a report can stand a little help. Here is a report on the current year-to-date selling efficiency that refers to a graph that provides the background of the last 12 month's behavior.

Strong

	A	B	C	D	E	F	G	H
44								
45		12-Jun-90	SALES AND SELLING COSTS, MONTH OF MAY					
46		January	February	March	April	May	June	July
47	Sales	16.00	20.00	21.00	27.00	27.00	0.00	0.00
48	Costs	5.50	5.50	5.50	6.00	6.00	0.00	0.00
49	Costs as % of sales	34%	28%	26%	22%	22%	0%	0%
50	Smoothed(5 mth)*							
51	Sales	21.4	22	22.2	25	27	0	0
52	Costs as % of sales	26%	25%	25%	24%	22%	0%	0%
53								
54	*Next to last month is smoothed over 3 months, last month is unsmoothed.							
55								
56	Note: This report is supported by the graph "Selling costs (%) down slightly in							
57	the last six months."							
58								

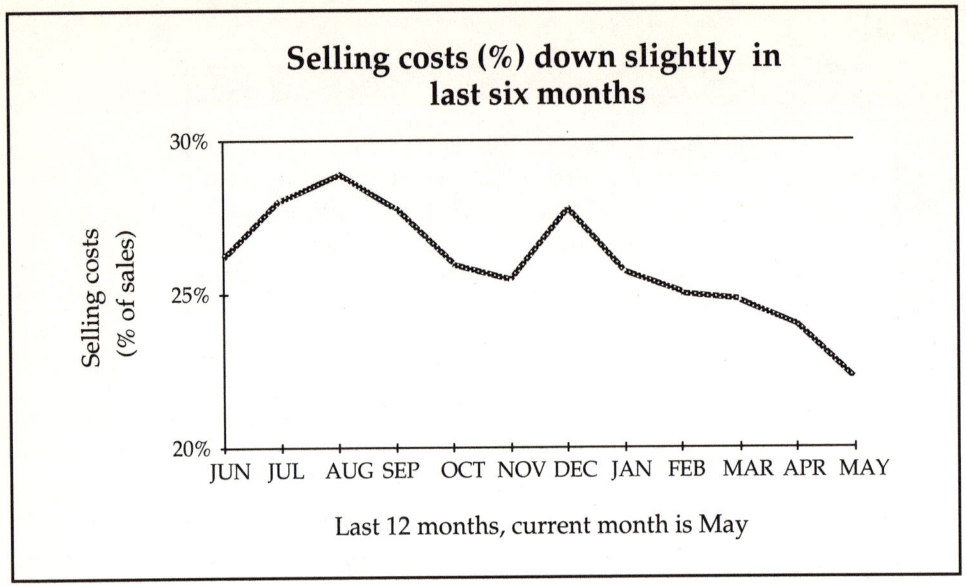

Here the graph backs up the report's information on the first five months of the current year with the trend for the last 12 months. Note that the author of the graph tells the reader in the title what the important point of the graph is: "Selling costs (%) down slightly in the last six months." Sometimes a small detail can add a lot to a report. Notice the use of asterisks in the next two examples, the same report in June and again in August.

Strong

	A	B	C	D	E	F	G	H	I	J	K
22	10-Jul-35	PERFORMANCE THROUGH MONTH OF JUNE									
23		Quarterly performance					Half performance			Year	
24		***	***	+++	+++		******	++++++		******++++++	
25		Qtr 1	Qtr 2	Qtr 3	Qtr 4		Half 1	Half 2		To date	To end
26	Planned	44	46	54	72		90	126		90	216
27	Actual	47	44	0	0		91	0		91	91
28		---------	---------	---------	---------		---------	---------		---------	---------
29	Ahead (behind)	3	(2)	--	--		1	--		1	(125)
30	% of plan	107%	96%	0%	0%		101%	0%		101%	42%
31		---									

Strong

	A	B	C	D	E	F	G	H	I	J	K
22	10-Sep-35		PERFORMANCE THROUGH MONTH OF AUGUST								
23		Quarterly performance					Half performance			Year	
24		***	***	**+	+++		******	**++++		********++++	
25		Qtr 1	Qtr 2	Qtr 3	Qtr 4		Half 1	Half 2		To date	To end
26	Planned	44	46	54	72		90	126		129	216
27	Actual	47	44	41	0		91	41		132	132
28		---------	---------	---------	---------		---------	---------		---------	---------
29	Ahead (behind)	3	(2)	(13)	--		1	(85)		3	(84)
30	% of plan	107%	96%	76%	0%		101%	33%		102%	61%
31		--					--				

The asterisks reinforce visually how much data are being reported. In June, all of the quarter, and all of the half—six months of the year. In August, two-thirds of a quarter, two-sixths of the second half, eight months of the year. The asterisks illustrate what it means to have completed the year through June, and in the second example, through August. A report can help the reader by providing no more numerical accuracy than is warranted.

Strong

	A	B	C	D	E	F	G
58	26-Nov-40 ESTIMATED PROJECT COMPLETION TIME						
59							
60	6	Number of activities on the project critical path					
61	137.5	Project mean completion time (50-50 chance)					
62	28.0	Project completion time standard deviation					
63							
64			PROJECT COMPLETION TIME TABLE				
65	Time:	54	102	114	123	131	138
66	Probability:	~0%	10%	20%	30%	40%	50%
67							
68	Time:	138	144	152	161	173	221
69	Probability:	50%	60%	70%	80%	90%	~100%
70							
71	---						

The report includes one decimal place when showing the project mean and standard deviation, but when it gets to the table of days, the numbers are rounded off to realistic whole days. In a 138-day project, it would be silly to talk about tenths of a day. The extra accuracy in the mean and standard deviation allows the reader, by consulting a table of normal distribution figures, to verify independently that the calculations in the time table are correct. The table itself allows the user to see quickly that the job will be done in 138 days, plus or minus 28 days. If the person doing the estimate is new, then the reader can assume the project will probably run long.

When a report draws on data in more than one submodel, the report area can become a submodel in its own right. The last submodel in the spreadsheet NEWBUD is a report. (See the discussion in Chapter 5 for a full explanation of the next example.)

Strong

	A	B
303		20-Jan-10
304	Corporate Financial Ratios	
305		
306	Asset turnover	2.07
307	Profit as a % of sales	9.6%
308	Return on assets	19.8%
309	Return on equity	16.2%
310	================================	

The report itself is terse. It will be included in an annual report where the surrounding text will explain the importance of the ratios. Knowing the context of a report affects what goes into it. Because Lotus 1-2-3 Release 3 allows each page of a spreadsheet to have a different set of column widths, be sure to use a separate page when a report requires varied column widths to improve its looks.

Graph to Illuminate

A graph seeks to shed light on fundamental ideas. Some graphs brilliantly summarize enormous amounts of data. Some pictorially represent a few simple numbers for an important reader who must be made aware of the numbers' importance. Most are concerned with the pattern of things, sales over time, markets over regions, variables causing other variables to do something, parts of the whole, the general line in the cloud of particular points. A picture, however, is not always worth a thousand words. In fact, some pictures require a thousand words before they make sense. If you would have your pictures speak for you, be clear about what you want them to say.

Your job is to be sure you are presenting the pattern in a way that elicits the proper response from your reader. An effective graph achieves the appropriate reaction from the reader. A graph is a special kind of report; a short checklist can help you to remember the essentials:

1. Lay it out in a familiar style: Conform to department practices.

2. Lay it out in an appealing style: Seduce the viewer's eye.

3. Put your major conclusion in your title.

4. Have the reader proofread the graph for content and format before it becomes official.

Because computer graphing allows heretofore difficult graphing to be done quickly and easily, you will find you are pioneering with new forms when you do some of your graphs. If you are breaking new ground, be careful to do a good job with your graphs. Well received graphs have a way of becoming the standard, and you will help everyone if your candidates for standards are the best possible pictures.

The foundation of a good graph is the appropriate data in the proper arrangement. In order to ensure this arrangement, you should establish a graphing area in your spreadsheets and base your charts and graphs on this area. The effort you expend to set up the area will be repaid in the freedom you achieve to draw the right graph.

Strong

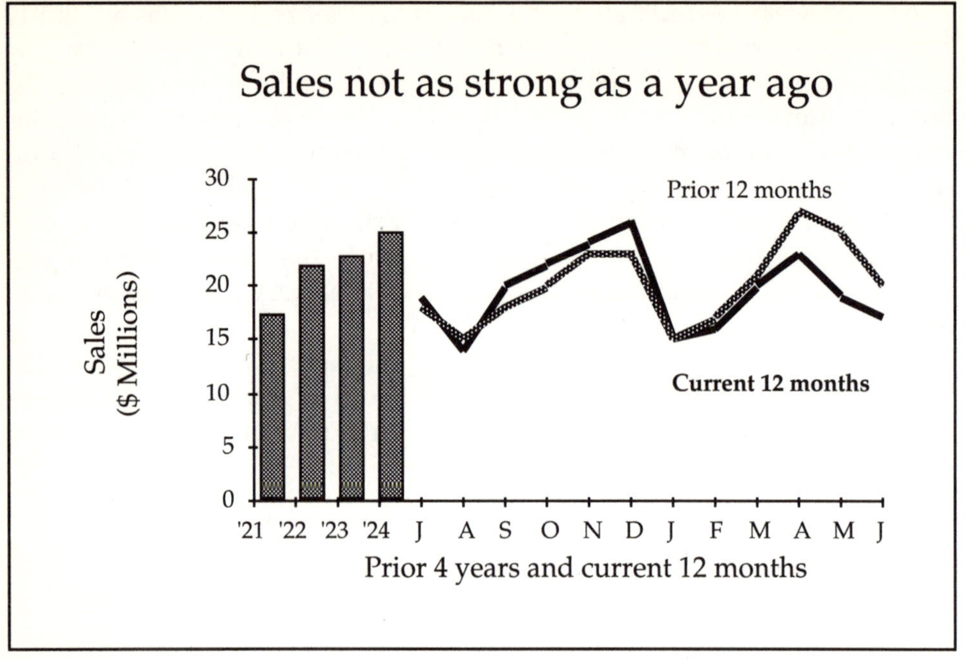

Here's a graph that conveys a large amount of information in a small area. It shows what the most recent 12 months of data are: cyclic in nature with highs in December and April. The long-term trend can be inferred from the past years' bars: Sales are up over several years (1621–1624). A recent problem is highlighted by the comparison with the prior 12-months' data: Recent sales are off. The main point the author wants to make is explicitly stated in the title of the graph: "Sales are not as strong as a year ago."

By establishing a graphing section, SALES gives you the freedom to do several things. First, you can make a row of labels for the x-axis that appears just the way you want it to. You could alter the labels to be the full names of the months that begin the year's quarters, January, April, July, and October. Because you are working in the graphing section, you know you are not messing up a printed report when you fiddle with the month names.

Strong

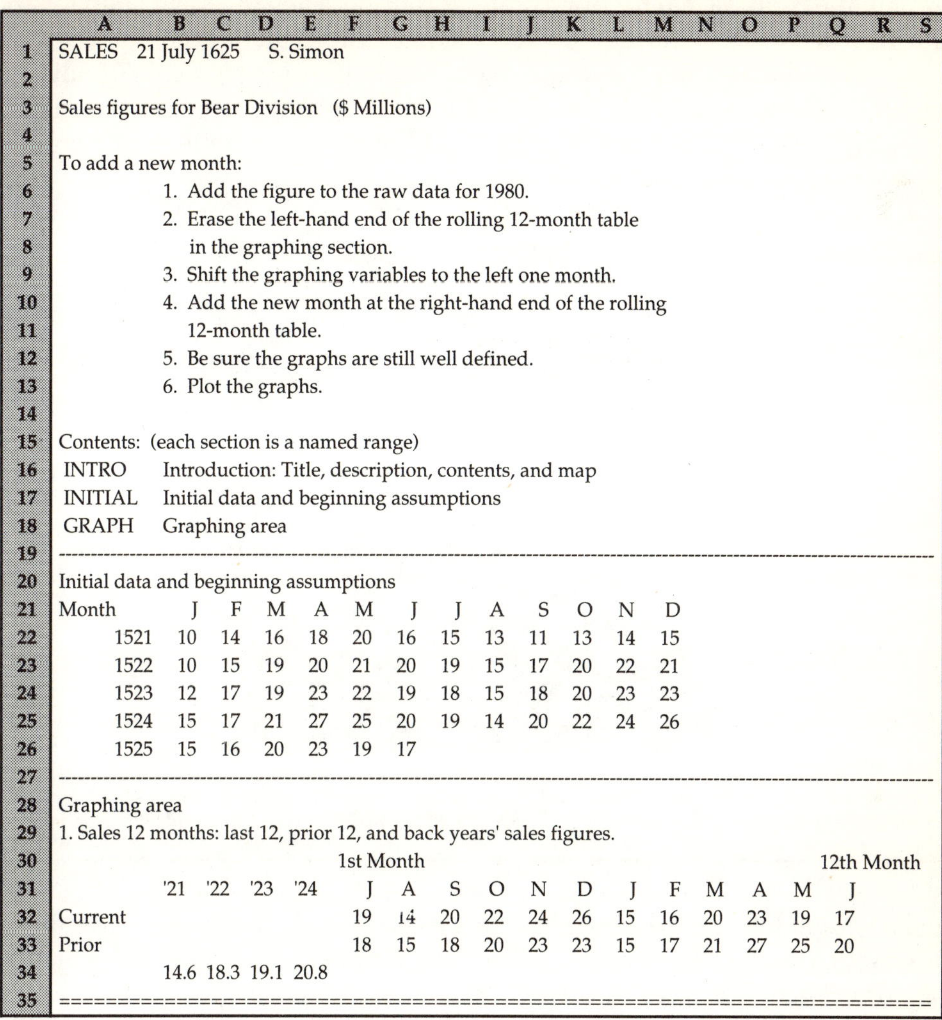

```
        A    B   C   D   E   F   G   H   I   J   K   L   M   N   O   P   Q   R   S
 1  SALES   21 July 1625     S. Simon
 2
 3  Sales figures for Bear Division   ($ Millions)
 4
 5  To add a new month:
 6              1. Add the figure to the raw data for 1980.
 7              2. Erase the left-hand end of the rolling 12-month table
 8                 in the graphing section.
 9              3. Shift the graphing variables to the left one month.
10              4. Add the new month at the right-hand end of the rolling
11                 12-month table.
12              5. Be sure the graphs are still well defined.
13              6. Plot the graphs.
14
15  Contents:  (each section is a named range)
16   INTRO      Introduction: Title, description, contents, and map
17   INITIAL    Initial data and beginning assumptions
18   GRAPH      Graphing area
19  -------------------------------------------------------------------------------
20  Initial data and beginning assumptions
21  Month         J   F   M   A   M   J   J   A   S   O   N   D
22        1521   10  14  16  18  20  16  15  13  11  13  14  15
23        1522   10  15  19  20  21  20  19  15  17  20  22  21
24        1523   12  17  19  23  22  19  18  15  18  20  23  23
25        1524   15  17  21  27  25  20  19  14  20  22  24  26
26        1525   15  16  20  23  19  17
27  -------------------------------------------------------------------------------
28  Graphing area
29  1. Sales 12 months: last 12, prior 12, and back years' sales figures.
30                                1st Month                              12th Month
31           '21  '22  '23  '24    J   A   S   O   N   D   J   F   M   A   M   J
32  Current                       19  14  20  22  24  26  15  16  20  23  19  17
33  Prior                         18  15  18  20  23  23  15  17  21  27  25  20
34          14.6 18.3 19.1 20.8
35  ============================================================================
```

Second, you can maintain a rolling 12-month graph without disturbing the convenient format of the raw data. A rolling 12-month graph could be a major inconvenience to a person who was maintaining a graph drawn on the raw data. By establishing graphing area, you allow the data to be manipulated in a convenient way from month to month, so that the spreadsheet can continue being useful after it has been turned over to someone else to use.

Third, you can assemble the information for the average annual bars in exactly the right format for our graphing routine. These average annual bars illustrate how a demanding format for a final graph can be accommodated if you allow yourself the freedom of a separate graphing area. Without the separate graphing area you might not even believe it possible to construct this graph. The separate area allows you to push on the limits of the graphing tools at your disposal.

The next example illustrates that the graphing area may be the home of special calculations necessary to produce the right picture.

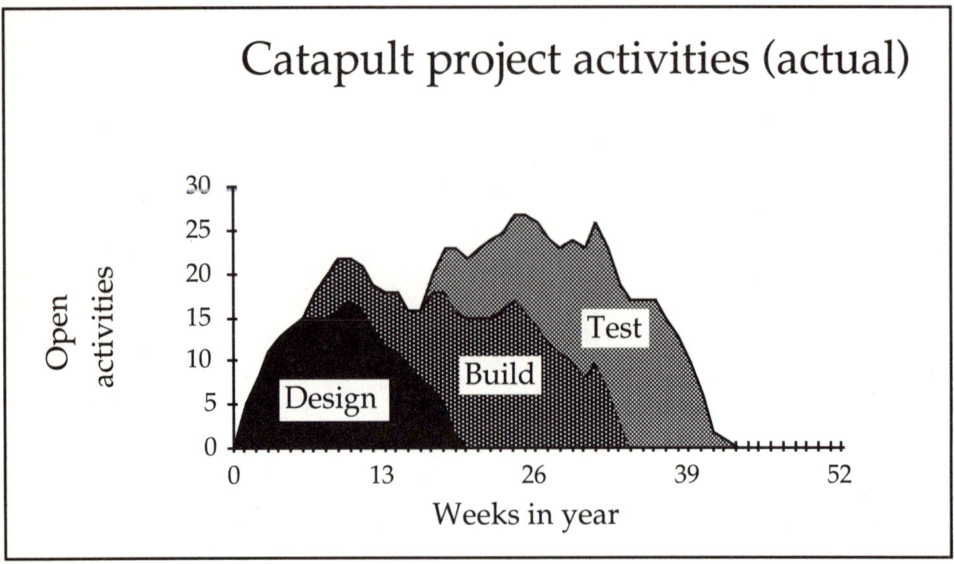

The graph tells a story about building a catapult. Activities were classified as design, build, or test activities. The total number of activities open at any one time was never greater than 27. When the project began, everyone was designing the catapult. In the sixth week some building activity started. By the seventeenth week building was going full swing, a little late design was being finished up, and a little early testing of some components was beginning. Testing and building went on together, with testing becoming the dominant activity by the thirty-third week. The last weeks were exclusively given over to completing the testing, which occurred during the forty-third week.

The graph depends on the number of open activities. This number depends in turn upon the difference between the cumulative number of activities opened and closed. The graphing area looks like this:

Strong

	A	B	C	D	E	F	G	H	I	J	K	L	M	N	O	P	...
52	Graphing area																
53																	
54	Graphs include:																
55	1. "Catapult project activities (actual)"																
56	2. "Total activity"																
57	Cumulative counts																
58	Week number	1	2	3	4	5	6	7	8	9	10	11	12	13	14	15	...
59	Design activities																
60	Assigned	5	11	18	25	32	40	47	53	59	64	68	72	75	78	81	...
61	Completed	0	3	7	12	18	25	32	38	43	47	52	58	63	67	71	...
62	Build activities																
63	Assigned	0	0	0	0	0	0	3	7	12	16	20	25	31	38	43	...
64	Completed	0	0	0	0	0	0	0	2	6	11	15	20	25	31	37	...
65	Test activities																
66	Assigned	0	0	0	0	0	0	0	0	0	0	0	0	0	0	0	...
67	Completed	0	0	0	0	0	0	0	0	0	0	0	0	0	0	0	...
68	Total activities																
69	Assigned	5	11	18	25	32	40	50	60	71	80	88	97	106	116	124	...
70	Completed	0	3	7	12	18	25	32	40	49	58	67	78	88	98	108	...
71																	
72																	
73	Open activities																
74	Week axis label	0	1	2	3	4	5	6	7	8	9	10	11	12	13	14	...
75	Design	0	5	8	11	13	14	15	15	15	16	17	16	14	12	11	...
76	Build	0	0	0	0	0	0	0	3	5	6	5	5	5	6	7	...
77	Test	0	0	0	0	0	0	0	0	0	0	0	0	0	0	0	...
78																	
79	Total (check)	0	5	8	11	13	14	15	18	20	22	22	21	19	18	18	...

Again, you see how the separate graphing area provides the necessary freedom to arrange the information in an appropriate manner for the proper pictures. The graph names are listed at the beginning of the Graphing Area. Notice that some simple formulas lurk behind the figures in the Graphing Area. The cumulative figure is the prior cumulative figure plus the current week's value. Open activities are the difference between cumulative assigned and cumulative completed. At some point, if the number and complexity of the formulas increased, they might be separated into a Model Area where they could be arranged so they would be easier to understand.

The next graph discloses an underlying pattern not obvious in the raw numbers.

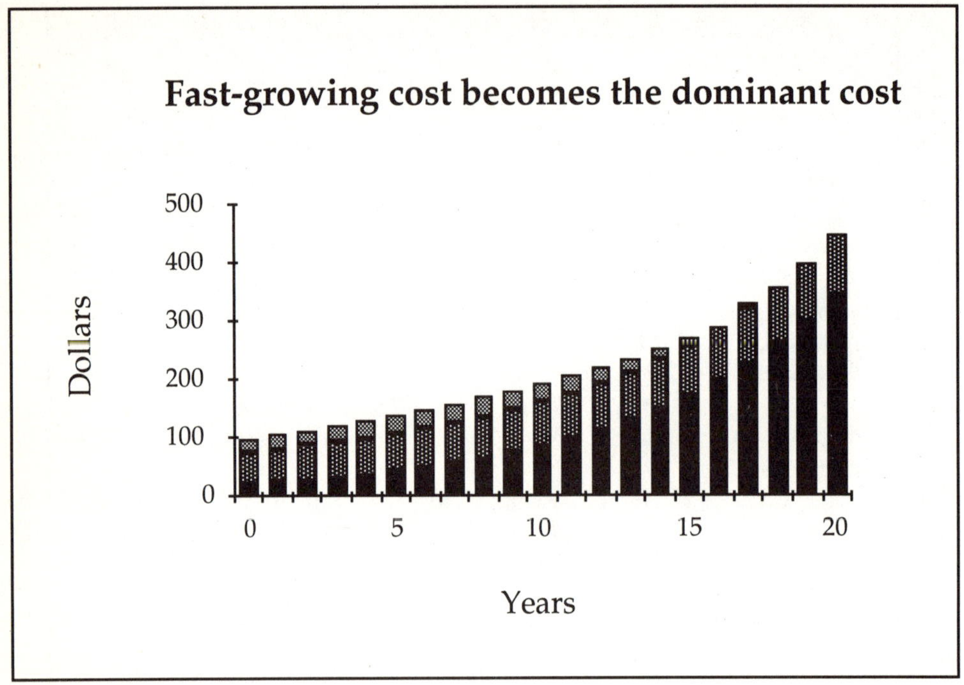

This chart from the model INFLATE shows how the initially small cost—labor—grows to dominate the cost structure of the product. In order to maintain a profit the price must follow the high growth cost component more closely as it becomes the dominant cost. In the above example, a 6.8 percent price growth rate leads to losses beginning in the seventeenth year. The point of the graph is spelled out in its title, "Fast-growing cost becomes the dominant cost." The pattern that is clear in the graph is hidden in the table of numbers.

	A	B	C	D	E	F	G
85	Graphing Section						
86							
87	YEAR	MATERIAL	LABOR	TOTL COST	PRICE	PROFIT	MARGIN
88	0	56	21	77	100	23	23.0%
89		58	24	82	107	25	23.4%
90		59	28	87	114	27	23.6%
91		61	32	93	122	29	23.6%
92		63	37	100	130	31	23.4%
93	5	65	42	107	139	32	23.0%
94		67	49	115	149	33	22.4%
95		69	56	125	159	34	21.5%
96		71	64	135	170	35	20.3%
97		73	74	147	181	34	18.9%
98	10	75	85	160	194	33	17.3%
99		78	98	175	207	32	15.3%
100		80	112	192	221	29	13.1%
101		82	129	211	236	25	10.5%
102		85	149	233	252	19	7.5%
103	15	87	171	258	270	11	4.2%
104		90	197	286	288	2	0.5%
105		93	226	319	308	-11	-3.6%
106		95	260	355	329	-27	-8.1%
107		98	299	397	351	-46	-13.1%
108	20	101	344	445	375	-70	-18.6%

A reader looking at this table of numbers would stare at it for several days before seeing the pattern of labor costs that leaps to the eye in the graph. The graph illuminates the important idea.

Sometimes a very simple chart can help explain position. The following chart tells a department how things are going two months through the quarter. This information is very interesting to people whose bonuses ride on making the goals.

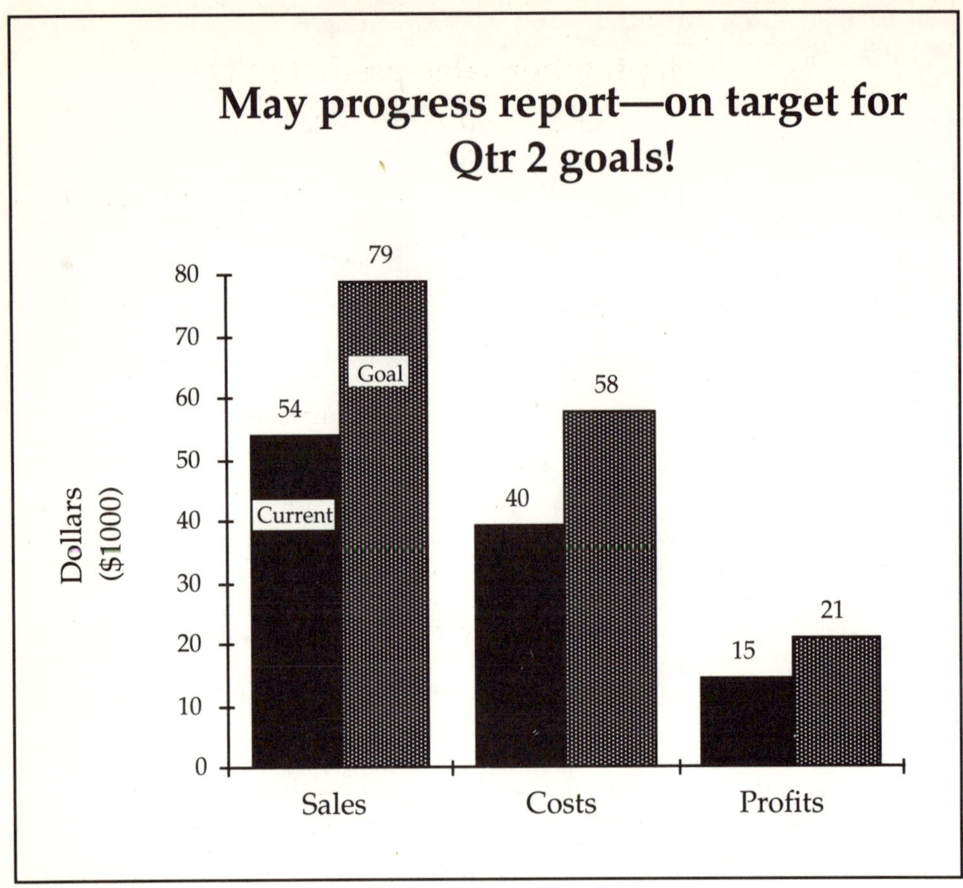

While this graph contains very little information and might justifiably be considered a poor graph for most purposes, it is an excellent chart to post on the wall to tell everyone what has been done, and what remains to be done, to hit the quarterly goals. During the final month, someone could pencil in progress on the chart.

The next example shows how a graph can present a great deal in a small space.

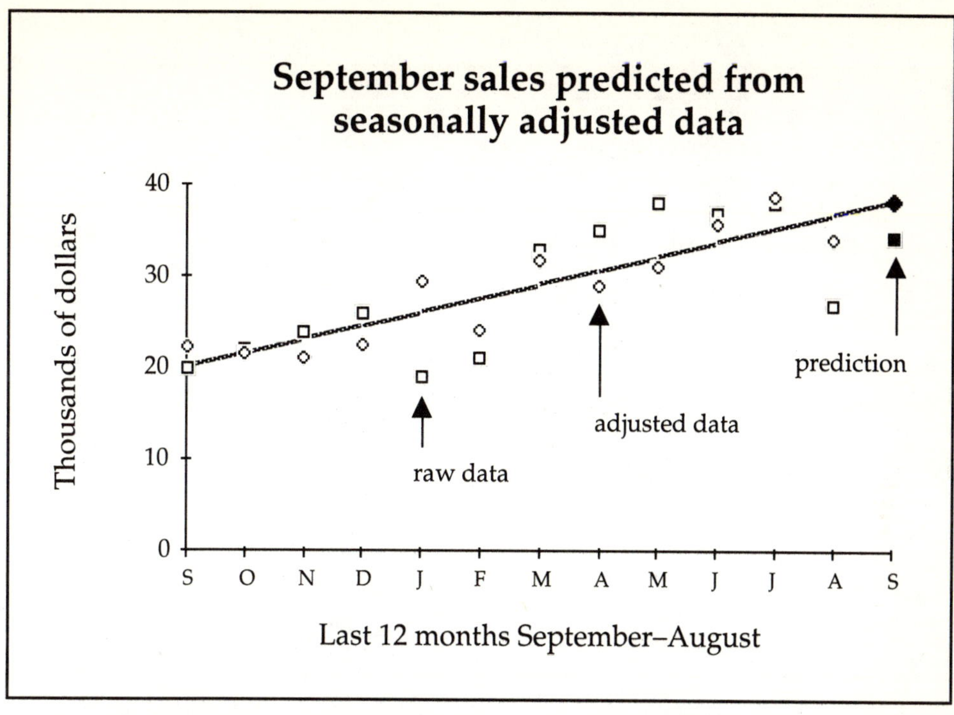

This chart shows the raw data of the last 12 months, the seasonally adjusted data of the same period, the best-fit line to the seasonally adjusted data, the projected value for the next month, and the predicted raw value. It is a good graph because it condenses lots of information into a compact, meaningful whole.

The portion of the graphing area on which the graph was based looks like this:.

Strong

	A	B	C	D	E	F	G
99	Graphing section:						
100	1. "September sales predicted from seasonally adjusted data"						
101	2. "Seasonal factors"						
102	Next month's sales						
103	x-label	x(i)	y(i)	s(i)	Line	s(13)	y(13)
104	S	1	20	22.3	20.1		
105	O	2	22	21.5	21.6		
106	N	3	24	21.2	23.1		
107	D	4	26	22.5	24.6		
108	J	5	19	29.4	26.2		
109	F	6	21	24.1	27.7		
110	M	7	33	31.9	29.2		
111	A	8	35	29.0	30.7		
112	M	9	38	31.2	32.3		
113	J	10	37	35.7	33.8		
114	J	11	38	38.7	35.3		
115	A	12	27	34.1	36.8		
116	S	13			38.4	38.4	34.4

Again you see a list of the graphs by name and a column of labels set up to help the graph. Notice also that the area uses a whole column to get s(13) and y(13) on the graph exactly the way it wants.

Sometimes a large amount of data can be reduced to a series of graphs that tell a story. The next three graphs summarize a model with over 330 equations. The model lets three firms compete for a growing market for ten years. Firm A wants to capture a large share of the market, Firm B wants to preserve its initial one third of the market, and Firm C is willing to give up share in exchange for a few year's of high prices. All three firms begin at the same place.

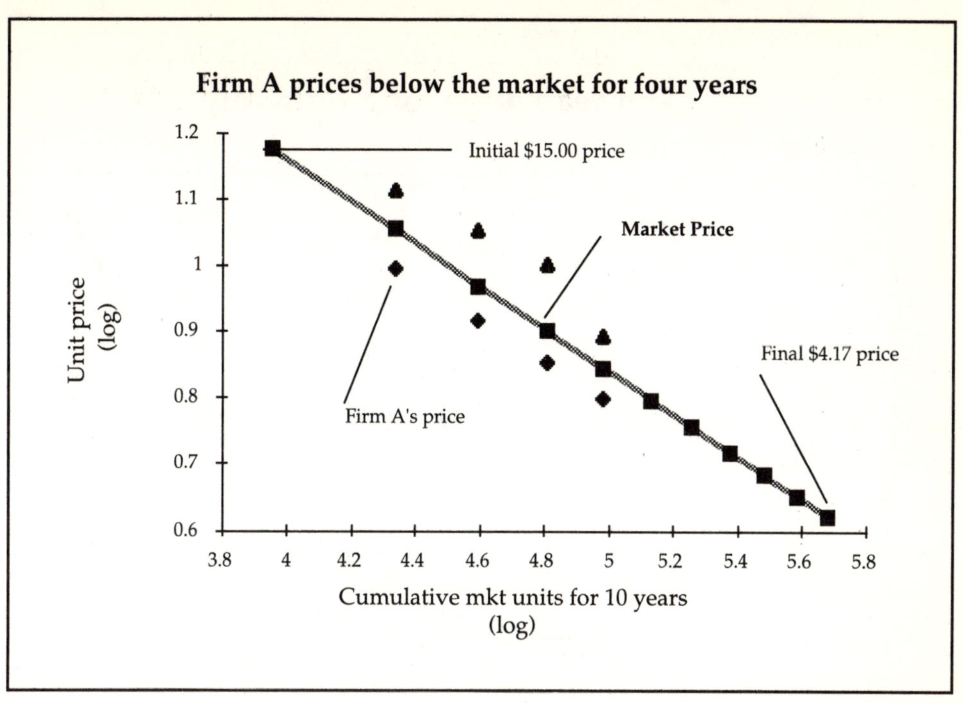

Firm A prices below the market for four years
Initial $15.00 price
Market Price
Firm A's price
Final $4.17 price
Unit price
(log)
Cumulative mkt units for 10 years
(log)
1.2
1.1
1
0.9
0.8
0.7
0.6
3.8
4
4.2
4.4
4.6
4.8
5
5.2
5.4
5.6
5.8

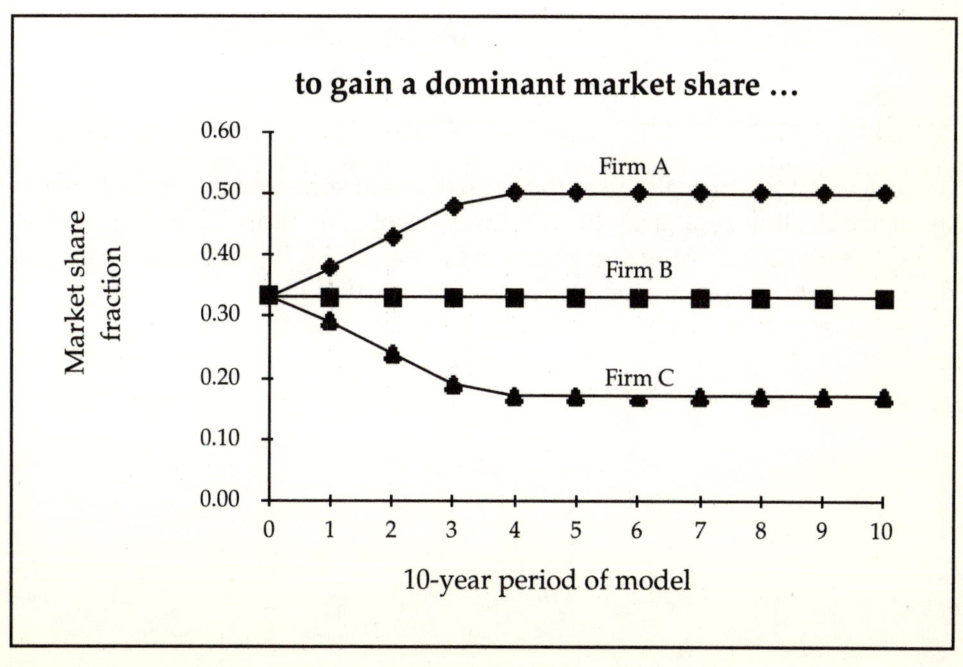

to gain a dominant market share ...
Firm A
Firm B
Firm C
Market share
fraction
0.60
0.50
0.40
0.30
0.20
0.10
0.00
0
1
2
3
4
5
6
7
8
9
10
10-year period of model

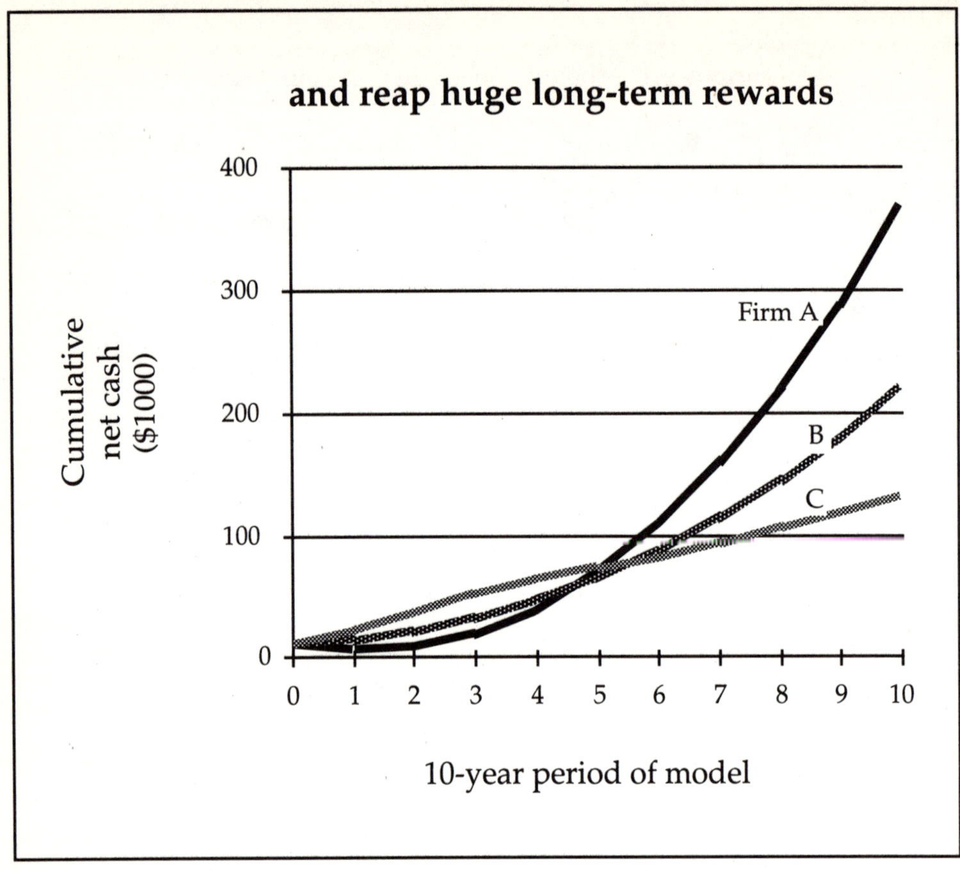

Notice that the first plot uses the logarithms of some data in order to show the price decline as a straight-line function of the cumulative market volume. The place where the logarithms are computed is in the graphing area. If data that you graph can be more clearly revealed if you transform it, the graphing area will give you a place to do your transformations.

Strong

	A	B	C	D	E	F	G	H	I
80	GRAPHING AREA								
81	1. "Firm pricing" — three firms in the market								
82	2. "Market share" — three firms market share over 10 years								
83	3. "Cumulative cash" — three firms 10 year net cash								
84			Price			log(price)		Cumulative		
85	Year	Firm A	Firm B	Firm C	Firm A	Firm B	Firm C	Market	Log(mkt)
86	0	15.00	15.00	15.00	1.18	1.18	1.18	9,000	3.95
87	1	9.93	11.43	13.01	1.00	1.06	1.11	21,600	4.33
88	2	8.25	9.34	11.28	0.92	0.97	1.05	39,240	4.59
89	3	7.15	7.98	10.08	0.85	0.90	1.00	63,936	4.81
90	4	6.72	7.00	7.82	0.83	0.85	0.89	96,041	4.98
91	5	6.28	6.28	6.28	0.80	0.80	0.80	134,567	5.13
92	6	5.71	5.71	5.71	0.76	0.76	0.76	180,797	5.26
93	7	5.24	5.24	5.24	0.72	0.72	0.72	236,275	5.37
94	8	4.84	4.84	4.84	0.68	0.68	0.68	302,847	5.48
95	9	4.49	4.49	4.49	0.65	0.65	0.65	382,734	5.58
96	10	4.17	4.17	4.17	0.62	0.62	0.62	478,599	5.68

The next graph is a summary of information contained in a report shown earlier. The graph of project completion time shows much more about when the project will end.

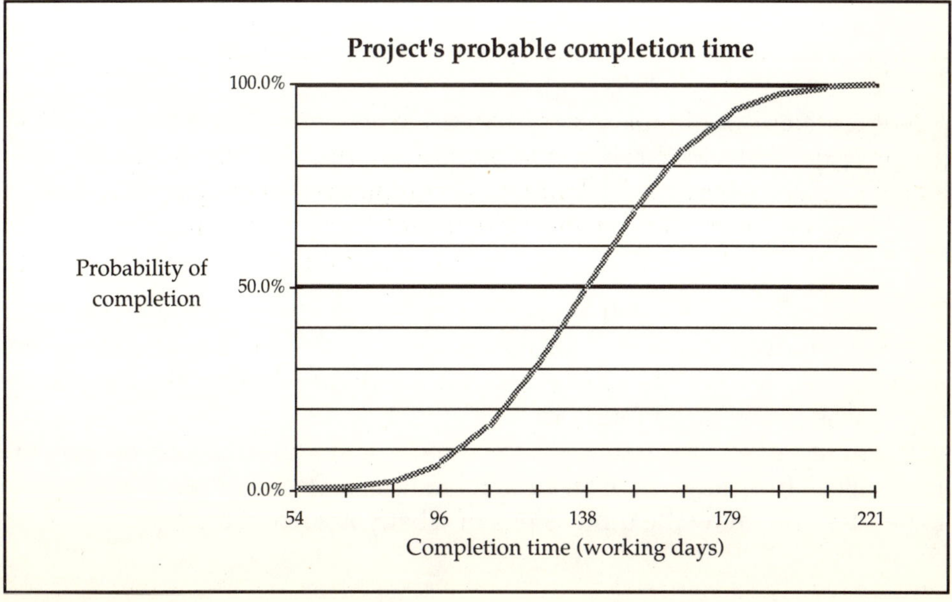

You can see at a glance that if you say you will be done in 179 days, you have more than a 90 percent chance of being right.

Because graphs make extraordinary first impressions, be sure to try out your graph on a real reader. Ask him or her to tell you what the point of the graph is. Revise your graph until it makes a first impression that is both powerful and correct.

Import with Care

When you move data between spreadsheets you are sometimes faced with the dilemma of importing a block of unknown size. A good way to import such a block is to land it on your spreadsheet to the right of your working model. Work imported in this location can be longer and wider than you anticipated and it will not damage your preexisting work. After you have landed the data safely, you may move it to its final resting place in your spreadsheet.

Even if your spreadsheet regularly receives a fixed block of information, set it down in your import area before moving it to its final location. This cautious practice will protect you against an unannounced change in size and give you a chance to catch someone else's oversight before it affects your work.

Because the import area is a temporary staging area for information destined to be moved elsewhere on your spreadsheet, it usually consists of two cells.

Strong

	G	H
1	Import area	
2		
3	XXXXXXX	

The XX cell is where you anchor the upper-left corner of the block. After you have moved the new information to its final resting place, erase any leftovers and reenter the XXs before you knock off work for the day. Leave the area as clean as you found it.

If you have 1-2-3 Release 3, always import onto a fresh page. You may export a block from anywhere on your spreadsheet. Do, however, take the time to be sure you know the dimensions of what you are exporting.

Verify Critical Work

When you build large models you will want to prove to yourself that everything is functioning properly. To be sure of your spreadsheet, you must verify critical work. A good way to guard against error is to build the model defensively by incorporating checks wherever possible.

A second reason to verify critical work is that you will want to be sure that any change you make in your program—changing a formula in the fifth column, erasing the fourth row, adding a new constant to the initial data—does not alter the important work of the model.

Verifying critical work springs from an attitude that has its roots in fourteenth century Italian traders who invented double-entry bookkeeping to be sure their accounts were in order. A modern-day accountant continues to ask whether the figures double check. Did you add the correct number of items? Was the sum correct? Did the row totals agree with the column totals? Was any number out of bounds by being either too large or too small?

In a spreadsheet model you can ask these questions with defensive formulas that have the following form:

(If everything is okay, print the answer, Otherwise print "error")
This expression can take many forms.

Weak	*Strong*
Positive number	Positive number
+A67	@IF(A67>=0,A67,@ERR)
Monthly salary	Monthly salary
+B20	@IF((B20>=1000)#AND#(B20<=30000),B20,@ERR)
Grand total of A1..S99	Grand Total of A1..S99
@SUM(A1..S99)	@IF(@SUM(T1..T99)=@SUM(A100..S100), @SUM(A1..S99),@ERR)
Sum of 100 Entries	Sum of 100 Entries
where the value 100 is in cell A5	where the value 100 is in cell A5
@SUM(A56..A155)	@IF(@COUNT(A56..A155)=A5,@SUM(A56..A155),@ERR)

You may think of these defensive formulas as warning lights. The positive number warning turns to error when the number goes negative. The monthly salary warning goes off when someone makes less than $12,000 a year or more than $360,000 a year. The grand total warning is triggered if the column of row totals does not cross check with the row of column totals. The sum of a fixed number (100) of entries is wrong if there are not exactly the right number of entries. (The fixed number is an initial datum stored in A5.)

Be careful with checks of equality and cross-checked sums in particular. Sometimes two sums will not be equal because of computer round-off error. The two totals will differ by a tiny amount that you will only see if you subtract the one quantity from the other. The difference may be as small as .00000000001. The safe way to ask if two numbers are equal is to ask if they differ by an insignificant amount. Because you won't know which is the bigger number, you should ask about the absolute value of the difference. If the absolute value of the difference is less than a tiny number, the numbers are "equal." The way to say that in a spreadsheet formula is:

> If (absolute value(sum – check sum) < .000001,
>   print sum, print "error")

Strong

Grand Total of A1..S99
@IF(@ABS(@SUM(T1..T99)–@SUM(A100..S100))<.000001,@SUM(A1..S99),@ERR)

The strong formula works in all cases where the difference is less than one part in a million. You may need to experiment to determine what small number is appropriate to your spreadsheet. If you are at all unsure what to use, ask someone who knows about computer round-off errors to help you.

You may be interested in only the relative error between two numbers. The formula for making sure the error is less that a tenth of a percent is:

> If (absolute value(1 – (sum/check sum)) < .001,
>   print sum, print "error")

In a large model, after you have established your warning lights, you may find it convenient to collect some of the critical lights into a "control panel" that will let you know quickly whether or not any of your warning lights have been set off. You may do this by establishing a Verify Area.

Strong

	A	B	C	D	E	F
14	Verify area					
15						
16	34470527 The model verification sum					
17						
18	If an error appears here, check below and then the appropriate area of the model.					
19	(Be sure you have recalculated the whole model.)					
20						
21	347000 The raw data cross check					
22	666352 The model cross check					
23	375 The number of items in the report					
24	33456777 The sum of all the checked values in the database					
25	23 The number of graphed periods					
26	---					

This Verify Area collects several warning lights in one place. If a cross check fails, an "error" appears in the individual listing and in the model verification sum. The verification sum is a nonsense number that uses the sum function as a quick way to detect if any item in the sum has gone bad.

Strong

	A	B	C	D	E	F
14	Verify area					
15						
16	ERR The model verification sum					
17						
18	If an error appears here, check below and then the appropriate area of the model.					
19	(Be sure you have recalculated the whole model.)					
20						
21	347000 The raw data cross check					
22	666352 The model cross check					
23	ERR The number of items in the report					
24	33456777 The sum of all the checked values in the database					
25	23 The number of graphed periods					
26	---					

In the above example, the verify sum model check is flashing "error." The individual item is from the report area. When you go to the Report Area, you will see the "error" warning there and you may correct the problem. Notice that the directions for the Verify Area include a reminder to recalculate the model before assuming that the warning lights are valid.

If you know of other corrective actions for your model, include them in the Verify Area.

Control All Macros

A macro can be a source of convenient help or a burden of confusing clutter. It is intended to help save typing time by allowing you to abbreviate several keystrokes to a single keystroke. A macro also allows the author of a model to simplify things for the eventual user. How much you engage in writing macros is directly related to who will be using the spreadsheet and how you want them to use it. On one hand, a macro can make possible an application that might otherwise be too time consuming. On the other hand, a macro must be expressed in a sloppy programming language that is fraught with perils. A macro will be useful only if you keep it under strict control.

The first level of control you should exhibit over macros is when to write one. Write as few macros as necessary. If you have a choice of making the spreadsheet clearer for the reader by documenting a feature or automating it with a macro, document it. Macros are hard to read; documentation is easy. The likelihood that the model will be reusable is much higher if you are clearly communicating with your reader.

The second level of control is to collect the macros you write in an area devoted to macros. Frequently this area will be at the bottom of the spreadsheet. Being at the bottom gets them out of harm's way. Here you may add additional length and not disturb the rest of the spreadsheet. If they appear in their own area, macros are more likely to be surrounded by appropriate comment. If you have 1-2-3 Release 3, **always** put the macro area on a separate page.

The third level of control is the documentation you bring to the macro. Macros are a frightfully terse form of expression. This imbues them with great power, but also with great mystery. To understand your own work, let alone to explain what you did to a second reader, requires careful attention to the detail of your comment.

Weak

	A
28	Macro area
29	
30	/fs~r

Strong

	A	B	C	D
32	Macro area			
33				
34		\R ~	Replace a file macro	
35		/fs~r		

The documentation here consists of two comments on either side of the macro's first cell which contains a tilde (~). The \R comment indicates that the cell to its right has a range name of \R. Without the \R comment on the left, the reader has no idea that the cell containing the tilde is the beginning of a macro called R. (Macros begin in cells with a two-character range name made up of a backslash (\) followed by a letter of the alphabet. If you do not understand macros, consult a guide to 1-2-3, Release 1A, to learn about the conventions employed here.) A reasonable style for range names is to always label the cell to the left of the one that is range named. Because of the left-hand range-name labels, a macro should go down column B. In addition to a range-name label, an explanatory comment can be placed in column A. When an extended remark is necessary, it can be placed on the same line, in a cell to the right of the macro command.

Weak

	A	B	C
37	Macro area		
38			
39		/dt1f13..i16~c3~	

Strong

	A	B	C	D
40	Macro area			
41				
42		\D ~	Data table definition	
43		/dt1DATATABLE1~INPUTCELL1~		

This example shows how a macro can save the settings for producing a table of summary data by saving the set of commands necessary to query the database. (See the 1-2-3, Release 1A, explanation of data tables.) With one keystroke you can invoke the first data table.

This example shows how a macro can create a feature that 1-2-3 lacks. The commands of 1-2-3 Release 1A allow you to save different combinations of settings for graphs, but do not allow you to save different settings for printing reports, or different settings for producing tables of summary data from databases. With this macro a single keystroke will invoke the first of what could be several different data tables.

The strong examples also illustrate the fourth, fifth, and sixth levels of control. They keep each line of macros short to aid both comprehension and editing. There is only one command on the line. These examples distinguish commands (lowercase) from areas acted upon (uppercase). They also use range names for all areas in the spreadsheet. The data table f13..i16 has been named DATATABLE1 and c3 has become INPUTCELL1. Range names preserve your freedom to move areas on your spreadsheet because range names move with the areas while cell names do not.

A seventh level of control is to keep the macro area under lock and key. The consequences of the inadvertent alteration of a single cell in this region can be calamitous. **Always** keep the Macro Area protected. Again, if you have 1-2-3 Release 3, always keep the Macro Area on a separate page.

The weak versus strong in the next example shows the cumulative effect of the above rules. Both versions do exactly the same thing. Only the strong version could be used by a second user, and only the strong version could be conveniently modified for extended reuse.

Weak

	A	B	C	D	E
44	Macro area				
45	Decision				
46		/xia27>10~True~			
47		False~			
48	Repetition				
49		/dfb33~1~~~			
50		/xib33>12~/xgb123~			
51		This line flashes with each repetition.~			
52		/re~			
53		/dfb33~b33+1~~~			
54		/xgb118~			
55		~			

Strong

	A	B	C	D	E
56	Macro area				
57		\A The decision (IF...THEN...ELSE) macro			
58		\B The repetition (DO WHILE) macro			
59					
60	Variables and constants				
61	COUNT	13			
62	HURDLE	10			
63	LIMIT	12			
64	VARIABLE	5			
65	----------------------				
66	This macro asks the question "Is the variable larger than the hurdle?"				
67	\A	~		This is a decision structure.	
68	IF	/xiVARIABLE>HURDLE~/xgIFTRUE~			
69		/xgIFFALSE~			
70	IFTRUE	~			
71		True~			
72		/xgIFEND~			
73	IFFALSE	~			
74		False~			
75	IFEND	~			
76					
77	--				
78	This macro flashes a line until the count exceeds the limit.				
79	\B	~		This is a repetition structure.	
80	LOOPTOP	/dfCOUNT~1~~~			
81	LOOPBEGIN	/xiCOUNT>LIMIT~/xgLOOPEND~			
82		This line flashes with each repetition.~			
83		/re~			
84		/dfCOUNT~COUNT+1~~~			
85		/xgLOOPBEGIN~			
86	LOOPEND	~			

Notice that the Macro Area, like the Graph Area, contains a table of contents. If you add a new macro to your model every day, a table of contents at the beginning of the Macro Area helps you find the correct macro.

A fundamental result of computer science is that you can write every computer program with three logical forms: sequence, decision, and repetition. Every macro proceeds down the spreadsheet until it encounters a blank line which forces it to stop (sequence). The above example, by illustrating the programming structures IF...THEN...ELSE (decision) and DO...WHILE (repetition), demonstrates that you can write regular computer programs with macro instructions.

1-2-3 Release 2 revised and improved the language of macros. These revisions were largely preserved unaltered in Release 3. The range name IF was changed to IFF to avoid conflicting with the command "if." The above example in the improved language looks like this:

Strong

	A	B	C	D	E	F
88	Macro area					
89		\A The decision (IF...THEN...ELSE) macro				
90		\B The repetition (DO WHILE) macro				
91						
92	Variables and constants					
93	COUNT	13				
94	HURDLE	10				
95	LIMIT	12				
96	VARIABLE	5				
97	----------------------					
98	This macro asks the question "Is the variable larger than the hurdle?"					
99	\A	~		This is a decision structure.		
100	IFF	{if VARIABLE>HURDLE} {branch IFTRUE}				
101		{branch IFFALSE}				
102	IFTRUE	~				
103		True~				
104		{branch IFEND}				
105	IFFALSE	~				
106		False~				
107	IFEND	~				
108						
109	---					
110	This macro flashes a line until the count exceeds the limit.					
111	\B	~		This is a repetition structure.		
112	LOOPTOP	{let COUNT;1}				
113	LOOPBEGIN	{if COUNT>LIMIT}{branch LOOPEND}				
114		This line flashes with each repetition.~				
115		/re~				
116		{let COUNT;COUNT+1}				
117		{branch LOOPBEGIN}				
118	LOOPEND	~				

By relying on commands in the language you can reduce the chances for careless mistakes. A stronger alternative of the repetition structure would let the language do the counting by using a {for} command, a subroutine (called LOOPBODY in the following example), and a {return} command. It might look like this:

Stronger

	A	B	C	D	E	F
120	Macro area					
121		\B The repetition (DO WHILE) macro				
122						
123	Variables and constants					
124	COUNT		13			
125	LIMIT		12			
126	--					
127	This macro flashes a line until the count exceeds the limit.					
128		\B	~		This is a repetition structure.	
129	LOOPBEGIN	{for COUNT;1;LIMIT;1;LOOPBODY}				
130		{branch LOOPEND}				
131	LOOPBODY	This line flashes with each repetition.~				
132		/re~				
133		{return}				
134	LOOPEND	~				

Should you need a loop to go on for a long time until some condition is met, make the upper limit very large and include an {if} command and a {forbreak} command in the loop body. For example, if you wanted to continue doing a loop until the user types "S" (for stop), the loop might look like this:

Strong

	A	B	C	D	E
136	Macro area				
137		\B The repetition (DO WHILE) macro			
138					
139	Variables and constants				
140	ANSWER	xx			
141	COUNT	13			
142	LIMIT	999999			
143	--				
144	This macro flashes a line until the user types an "S".				
145	\B	~	This is a repetition structure.		
146	LOOPBEGIN	{for COUNT;1;LIMIT;1;LOOPBODY}			
147		{branch LOOPEND}			
148	LOOPBODY	{get ANSWER}			
149		{if @upper(ANSWER)="S"} {forbreak}			
150		This line flashes with each repetition.~			
151		/re~			
152		{return}			
153	LOOPEND	~			

The strong examples all illustrate another feature of good programming: Each logical form has a single beginning cell and a single ending cell. This enables these forms to appear in a sequence, do their work and return to the sequence when they are done. The sequence could be inside a repetition or inside a branch of a decision. These forms can be embedded inside one another to create larger forms. Decisions can occur inside loops, and loops can occur inside branches of a decision. If you were to make repeated use of an IF structure, the first set of range names could be IFF1, IFTRUE1, and so on. The second structure could begin IFF2, and so on.

Be sure to note in the strong examples that the cell containing the value 5 of VARIABLE and the cell containing the value 13 of COUNT must be unprotected so they may be changed without disabling the protection scheme that covers the rest of the Macro Area.

If you must write a lot of macros, be sure to consult Ridington and Tucker's *Inside Lotus 1-2-3 Macros* (see References at the back of this book). You should extend your control over macros by learning as much as you can about what computer programmers call structured programming and be able to apply it to writing your macros. If you find yourself writing many large macros, see a professional programmer for help.

The next macro allows the user to choose one of three graphs from a menu. The menu explanation tells whether the selection is line, bar, or pie. (See 1-2-3 Release 1A explanation of the /xm command.)

Weak

	A	B	C	D
155	/xmmenu~			
156	Tulip	Daffodil	Rose	Quit
157	line of tulip	bar of daffodil	pie of rose	quit
158	/gnutulip~q~	/gnudaffodil~q~	/gnurose~q~	/xq~
159	/xmmenu~	/xmmenu~	/xmmenu~	

Strong

	A	B	C	D	E
161	This macro allows the user to choose one of three graphs from a menu.				
162					
163	\M	~			
164		/xmMENU~			
165					
166	MENU	Tulip	Daffodil	Rose	Quit
167		line of tulip	bar of daffodil	pie of rose	quit
168		/gnuTULIP~q~	/gnuDAFFODIL~q~	/gnuROSE~q~	/xgENDMENU~
169		/xmMENU~	/xmMENU~	/xmMENU~	
170					
171	ENDMENU	~			

In the weak version when you quit the menu, the macro stops, but in the strong version the menu goes to its ending cell (named ENDMENU). Because the strong menu has a single beginning cell (named MENU) and a single ending cell (named ENDMENU), it can be entered from a larger macro and returned to that macro after it ends.

The above menu done in 1-2-3 Releases 2 and 3 macro commands would look like this:

Strong

	A	B	C	D	E
173	This macro allows the user to choose one of three graphs from a menu.				
174					
175	\M	~			
176		{menubranch MENU}			
177					
178	MENU	Tulip	Daffodil	Rose	Quit
179		line of tulip	bar of daffodil	pie of rose	quit
180		/gnuTULIP~q~	/gnuDAFFODIL~q~	/gnuROSE~q~	{branch ENDMENU}
181		{menubranch MENU}	{menubranch MENU}	{menubranch MENU}	
182					
183	ENDMENU	~			

A handy form for a menu macro that gives the user a little extra direction is the following (from Ridington and Tucker, p.386)

Strong

	A	B	C	D	E
185	This macro prompts the user to make a choice from a menu.				
186					
187	TOPMENU	{menubranch MENU}			
188					
189	MENU	Please choose:	Choice 1	Choice 2	Quit
190		Point to choice and press return	This is #1	This is #2	To quit menu
191		{branch TOPMENU}	{CHOICE1}	{CHOICE2}	{branch ENDMENU}
192			{branch TOPMENU}	{branch TOPMENU}	
193	ENDMENU	~			

The first thing that appears in the menu are two lines of directions. If the user inadvertently hits the return key, the menu is redisplayed. When the user makes a choice, a name enclosed in curly braces, such as {CHOICE1}, directs the program to go the routine called CHOICE1 and work there until a {return} command sends the program back. When the user is finished, "Quit" sends the program to the end of the menu structure.

You can easily use this menu form to construct a pyramid of menus and submenus. Because menus give you a way to write documentation that is familiar to the user, an eighth level of control over macros is to embed the macros in a macro menu. The first choice in the above example might change from "Tulip" to "Graphing Macros," and the actual example would be the first submenu. The second major choice might be "Database Macros," the third, "Printing Macros," and so on. The menus might be organized like this:

Macro menu organization
    Graphing menu
        Line graph of Tulip
        Bar chart of Daffodil
        Pie chart of Rose
    Database reports
        Workers by project
        Workers by week
        Projects by week
    Printed reports
        $8\,1/2 \times 11$ reports
            Report on workers
            Report on roses
        11×14 reports
            Report on projects and weeks
            Report on flowers

Should you find yourself this deeply involved in writing macros, seriously consider hiring a professional to help you with this part of your spreadsheet. Carefully distinguish between those macros you need and those you wish you needed. Always, always, control your macros.

Focus the Model's Activity

Sometimes a model is written so that a user can systematically vary one of the initial variables and observe the effects on a critical result that is at the far end of the spreadsheet. To look at both numbers easily the spreadsheet may be split into two windows. If, however, several widely dispersed results must be examined, the window solution becomes inconvenient. The way to resolve this problem is to define a new area, the Active Area. Treat the Active Area like an animated report that focuses the model's activity.

The Active Area is a dynamic area that collects in one place both the initial data to be manipulated and the final results to be watched. It should be attractively formatted to be easy to use.

Before beginning the day's activity, the author (or the user) can move the original initial data to the Active Area and leave behind formulas in the Initial Data Area that point to the Active Area. The user may then go to the Active Area, vary the initial variables to his or her heart's content, print out appropriate findings (the Active Area has been set up like a Report Area so the results are printable), and think about his or her findings. When the user is done, he or she restores the initial data to the original Initial Data Area (or throws away the active version of the spreadsheet) and quits for the day.

Strong

	A	B	C	D	E
195	Active area				
196					
197	MANPOWER COVERAGE OF SCHEDULED WORK FOR NEXT FOUR QUARTERS				
198					3 July 1586
199	23 Manpower available at end of current quarter				
200	2 Current quarter number				
201					
202	Scheduled work covered by current manpower				
203	Quarter	Work covered (%)			
204	3	87			
205	4	65			
206	5	110			
207	6	120			
208					

Here the user changes the number of people available and the quarter when they are available to see what percentage of the upcoming scheduled work will be covered. The user might decide to get more people and want to see what effect it has on the project:

Strong

	A	B	C	D	E
209	Active area				
210	MANPOWER COVERAGE OF SCHEDULED WORK FOR NEXT FOUR QUARTERS				
211					3 July 1586
212	25 Manpower available at end of current quarter				
213	2 Current quarter number				
214					
215	Scheduled work covered by current manpower				
216	Quarter	Work covered (%)			
217	3	92			
218	4	75			
219	5	130			
220	6	150			
221					

Strong

	A	B	C	D	E
222	Active area				
223	MANPOWER COVERAGE OF SCHEDULED WORK FOR NEXT FOUR QUARTERS				
224					3 July 1586
225		30 Manpower available at end of current quarter			
226		2 Current quarter number			
227					
228	Scheduled work covered by current manpower				
229	Quarter	Work covered (%)			
230		3	102		
231		4	90		
232		5	160		
233		6	175		
234					

From these trials the user chooses the last as a reasonable alternative. Note that this active area probably depends on a large, elaborately scheduled model that integrates all the projects the group is working on.

As a general rule, the model should be saved with the initial data in the Initial Data Area. If, however, a particular spreadsheet only exists to perform an Active Area chore, then the spreadsheet might be profitably rearranged with the Active Area at the top:

Strong

	A	B	C	D
5	Contents			
6		Introduction		
7		Active area		
8		Initial data		
9		Supporting model		
10		Occasional report		
11		Rarely used graphing area		

This arrangement provides the user with the convenience of quickly getting to the Work Area. The Active Area might also be saved in its active state. (But a note to warn the user should also be included in the Initial Data Area. For example, "WARNING: Some of the initial data are controlled from the Active Area.")

Strong

	A	B	C	D	E	F
32	Active area					
33						
34	GNP Growth, Unemployment, and Inflation as a Function					
35	of Monetary Growth(M1) and Fiscal Control(Natl. Debt).					15 Sept 1986
36						
37		Year 1	Year 2	Year 3	Year 4	Year 5
38	M1 growth	10.0%	15.0%	13.0%	11.0%	8.0%
39	Natl. Debt ($B)	240	160	90	60	0
40						
41	GNP growth	4.6%	7.6%	5.1%	3.2%	0.0%
42	Unemployment	6.7%	4.9%	4.3%	4.8%	6.8%
43	Inflation	4.6%	5.2%	7.5%	6.1%	4.5%
44	--					

This is an Active Area that a policy maker can use to manipulate different assumptions about the monetary (M1) growth rate and the national debt to see the effects on gross national product (GNP), unemployment, and inflation. The supporting spreadsheet may well contain pages of calculations, several different kinds of reports, and many charts and graphs. But what the policy maker needs to see, and occasionally needs to print out, are two key assumptions and three critical results. The Active Area provides just what is needed.

The impulse behind the Active Area is to give a casual user an easy way to manipulate the spreadsheet. If you pursue this impulse very far, you will find yourself using macros to prepare for the user, to guide the user through certain tasks, and to help the user end the session gracefully. You should consult a book on writing and using macros for help and guidance. If you combine the macro methods you learn there with well structured spreadsheets, you will provide the casual user with an industrial strength spreadsheet that will withstand heavy use.

Conclusion

Beyond the basic spreadsheet model, giving new functions new forms leads to an expanded set of areas. This chapter has discussed the most common forms, but you should not stop here. Create your own when you need to. The concluding example in this chapter, FULL RULE, contains all the areas and lists all the rules in each area.

Strong

	A	B	C	D	E	F	G	H	I
1	FULL RULE	17 July 1383	Mother Goose				Import area		
2		TITLE TO TELL					(move right before use)		
3	20-Feb-89	:Date printed					XXXXXXX		
4	(C) Copyright 1988 by John M. Nevison						IMPORT WITH CARE		
5		MAKE A FORMAL INTRODUCTION							
6	Provide a framework with which to begin building models.								
7		DECLARE THE MODEL'S PURPOSE							
8	To use: call it up, change its name, save it with its new name,								
9	and edit to your purpose.								
10		GIVE CLEAR INSTRUCTIONS							
11	Reference: John M. Nevison, "1-2-3 Spreadsheet Design,"								
12		New York, NY: Brady Books, 1989.							
13		REFERENCE CRITICAL IDEAS							
14	Contents: (each section is a named range in 1-2-3)								
15	INTRO	Introduction: Title, description, contents.					IMPORT	Import Area	
16	INITIAL	Initial data and beginning assumptions							
17	MODEL	Model							
18	REPORT	Report area							
19	GRAPH	Graph area							
20	VERIFY	Verify area							
21	ACTIVE	Active area							
22	MACRO	Macro area							
23	SUBMOD	Sample submodel							
24		MAP THE CONTENTS							
25	--								
26	Initial data and beginning assumptions								
27		IDENTIFY THE DATA							
28		SURFACE AND LABEL EVERY ASSUMPTION							
29	--								
30	Model								
31		MODEL TO EXPLAIN							
32		POINT TO THE RIGHT SOURCE							
33	--								
34		FIRST DESIGN ON PAPER							
35		TEST AND EDIT							
36		KEEP IT VISIBLE							
37		SPACE SO THE SPREADSHEET MAY BE EASILY READ							
38		GIVE A NEW FUNCTION A NEW AREA							
39	--								

(continued)

	A	B	C	D	E	F	G	H	I
40	Report area								
41		REPORT TO YOUR READER							
42	--								
43	Graph area								
44		GRAPH TO ILLUMINATE							
45	--								
46	Verify area								
47		VERIFY CRITICAL WORK							
48	--								
49	Active area								
50		FOCUS THE MODEL'S ACTIVITY							
51	--								
52	Macro area								
53		CONTROL ALL MACROS							
54	==								
55	Sample submodel								
56		ENTER CAREFULLY							
57	Initial data								
58	Data entering from another submodel								
59	--								
60	Submodel								
61	==								

If you chose to begin your spreadsheets with FULL RULE, you may avoid many sins of omission. Because you will be throwing away the areas you don't need you will not forget those you do need. The template also places a quick reminder of the rules in front of you. Beginning with good rules and appropriate areas will increase the speed and strength of your spreadsheet construction.

5

The Submodel

A CANDLE
Little Nanny Etticoat
In a white petticoat
And a red nose;
The longer she stands
The shorter she grows.

Sometimes a large spreadsheet gets out of control. Several areas of a large model can depend on each other in such complex ways that the model becomes hard to understand and difficult to modify. Sometimes the activities associated with one part of a model evolve more rapidly than the activities associated with the rest. Sometimes one part gets used in several different spreadsheets. Sometimes two or more old spreadsheets combine to make one effective new one. Sometimes a spreadsheet gets used by several individuals each of whom wants to control a part of the spreadsheet. Any one of these events could require the creation of a sound submodel.

If you own 1-2-3 Release 3, you have the ability to divide your spreadsheet into different pages. A properly constructed submodel will allow you to exploit this ability to split spreadsheets into pages and to form pieces that you can conveniently use and reuse.

Consider for a moment what you might do to break up a large, complex model into submodels. Converting such a model is a little like doing a condominium conversion on an apartment house—when you are finished you will have the same basic material, but each piece will have a certain independence from the others.

Before	*After*
Introduction	Introduction
Initial Data	Submodel 1
Data for part 1	Initial and Entering Data Area
Data for part 2	Model Area
Data for part 3	Report A
Model Area	Submodel 2
Part 1	Initial and Entering Data Area
Part 2	Model Area
Part 3	Submodel 3
Report A using Part 1	Initial and Entering Data Area
Report B using Parts 2 & 3	Model Area
Report C using 3	Report C
	Submodel 4
	Entering data
	Report B (using Submodels 2 & 3)

Notice that each independent submodel was created with an Initial and Entering Data Area. This new area is one of the results of the fundamental rule of the spreadsheet submodel.

Enter Carefully

Any cell of a spreadsheet can be used in a formula somewhere else. Because any cell can appear in a remote formula at any time, every spreadsheet area and submodel is completely vulnerable to unannounced exits. Because you cannot control a submodel's exits, you must control its entrances. You can do this by being sure that everything enters a submodel through its Initial and Entering Data Area.

Entering data can be controlled in a familiar way. Every basic spreadsheet controls data with its Initial Data Area and a submodel does the same. The reason entrances can be controlled is that they are of immediate interest to you, the author of the submodel. In order to see what the submodel depends on, you must establish an Initial and Entering Data Area. Without this, you cannot independently test the submodel and prove to yourself that it works. When you build a submodel, you must enter carefully.

The logic of spreadsheets asserts that exiting data is inherently unstable. Figure 5-1 depicts the outflow from Part 1 of a model. Even if you wished to control these exits by moving them to an Exit Area at the bottom of Part 1, the next undisciplined author who added a Part 4 could tap into your Part 1 at any point. The open nature of a spreadsheet renders exiting data impossible to control.

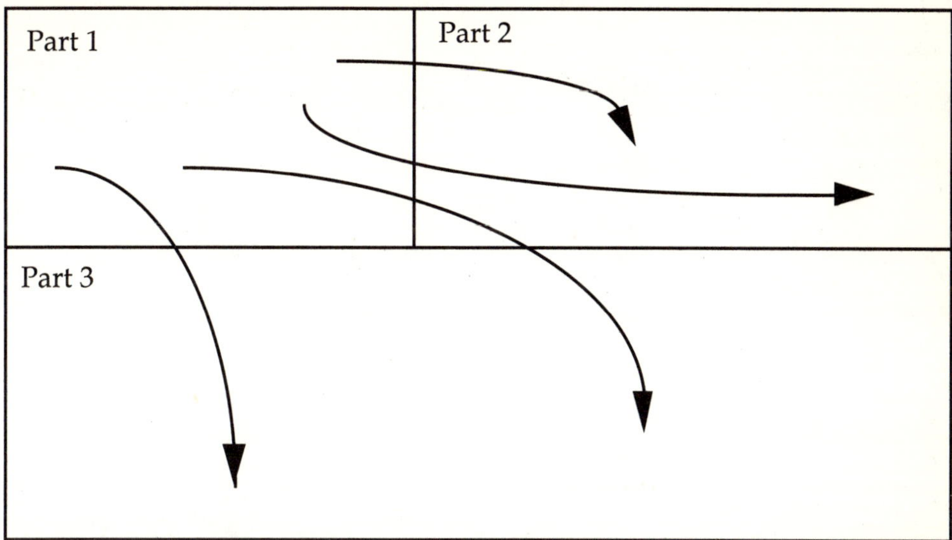

Figure 5-1. Uncontrolled exits from Part 1 occur when foreign formulas refer to cells in Part 1.

Notice that a spreadsheet gets larger when it is broken into submodels because all the entering data are labeled in a separate place for the first time. Submodels also disperse the control from one central location to several locations. In the next example, a kingdom's spreadsheet will be divided up among three castles.

	A	B	C	D	E	F	G
1	THREE CASTLE KINGDOM—Step 1						
2	Initial data						
3			Kings flag				
4			Stone				
5			Wood				
6			Red paint				
7			Yellow paint				
8			Black paint				
9	Castle Red						
10			Red walls = stone + red paint				
11			Red tower = yellow tower copy + stone + red paint				
12			Red drawbridge = black drawbridge copy + wood + red paint				
13			Red castle = red walls + red drawbridge + red tower + King's flag				
14	Castle Yellow						
15			Yellow walls = red wall copy + stone + yellow paint				
16			Yellow tower = stone + yellow paint				
17			Yellow drawbridge = black drawbridge copy + wood + yellow paint				
18			Yellow castle = yellow walls + yellow drawbridge + yellow tower + King's flag				
19	Castle Black						
20			Black walls = stone + black paint				
21			Black tower = yellow tower copy + stone + black paint				
22			Black drawbridge = wood + black paint				
23			Black castle = black walls + black drawbridge + black tower + King's flag				

In THREE CASTLE KINGDOM—Step 1, you see some of the model's data flows: from the initial data to the model (stone, wood), from one location in the initial data to many parts of the model (King's flag), from one part of the model to another (red wall copy), from one part of the model to many other parts (black drawbridge copy), and from many parts of the model to one part (Red castle formula).

Step 2 will show the evolution of a large model into three submodels.

	A	B	C	D	E	F	G
1	THREE CASTLE KINGDOM—Step 2						
2	Castle Red						
3	Initial data						
4		Kings flag					
5		Red paint					
6	Model						
7		Red walls = stone + red paint					
8		Red tower = yellow tower copy + stone + red paint					
9		Red drawbridge = black drawbridge copy + wood + red paint					
10		Red castle = red walls + red drawbridge + red tower + King's flag					
11	Castle Yellow						
12	Initial data						
13		Stone					
14		Yellow paint					
15	Model						
16		Yellow walls = red wall copy + stone + yellow paint					
17		Yellow tower = stone + yellow paint					
18		Yellow drawbridge = black drawbridge copy + wood + yellow paint					
19		Yellow castle = yellow walls + yellow drawbridge + yellow tower + King's flag					
20	Castle Black						
21	Initial data						
22		Wood					
23		Black paint					
24	Model						
25		Black walls = stone + black paint					
26		Black tower = yellow tower copy + stone + black paint					
27		Black drawbridge = wood + black paint					
28		Black castle = black walls + black drawbridge + black tower + King's flag					

Step 2 shows the intermediate partitioning of the model. Notice that here we have a problem with terms in formulas that come from other submodels (the copies of the drawbridge, stone, King's flag). These terms could be nearby or far away. They are not visible locally if you wanted to modify them. If you tried to extract one submodel from the spreadsheet, and remembered to freeze the values in the Initial Data Area, you would still find mysterious errors in the submodel's Model Area. For example, an extracted Castle Yellow would look like this:

Weak

	A	B	C	D	E	F	G
1	Castle Yellow (extracted from THREE CASTLE KINGDOM—Step 2)						
2	Initial data						
3		Stone					
4		Yellow paint					
5	Model						
6		Yellow walls = @ERR + stone + yellow paint					
7		Yellow tower = stone + yellow paint					
8		Yellow drawbridge = @ERR + @ERR + yellow paint					
9		Yellow castle = @ERR + @ERR + yellow tower + @ERR					

When a submodel is correctly extracted from a large spreadsheet, no error should occur. But when Castle Yellow's extracted submodel contains errors in the Model Area the submodel partitioning has serious problems. The last step resolves these problems.

	A	B	C	D	E	F	G
1	THREE CASTLE KINGDOM—Step 3						
2	Castle Red						
3	Initial and entering data						
4		King's flag					
5		Red paint					
6	From Castle Yellow						
7		Stone					
8		Yellow tower design					
9	From Castle Black						
10		Wood					
11		Black drawbridge design					
12	Model						
13		Red walls = stone + red paint					
14		Red tower = yellow tower copy + stone + red paint					
15		Red drawbridge = black drawbridge copy + wood + red paint					
16		Red castle = red walls + red drawbridge + red tower + King's flag					
17	Castle Yellow						
18	Initial and entering data						
19		Stone					
20		Yellow paint					
21	From Castle Red						
22		King's flag					
23		Red wall design					
24	From Castle Black						
25		Wood					
26		Black drawbridge design					

(continued)

	A	B	C	D	E	F	G
27	Model						
28		Yellow walls = red wall copy + stone + yellow paint					
29		Yellow tower = stone + yellow paint					
30		Yellow drawbridge = black drawbridge copy + wood + yellow paint					
31		Yellow castle = yellow walls + yellow drawbridge + yellow tower + King's flag					
32	Castle Black						
33	Initial and entering data						
34		Wood					
35		Black paint					
36	From Castle Red						
37		King's flag					
38	From Castle Yellow						
39		Stone					
40		Yellow tower design					
41	Model						
42		Black walls = stone + black paint					
43		Black tower = yellow tower copy + stone + black paint					
44		Black drawbridge = wood + black paint					
45		Black castle = black walls + black drawbridge + black tower + King's flag					

In the final step, the Initial and Entering Data Area distinguishes between new data that first appear in the submodel and old data that come from another submodel. For example, Castle Yellow has its own stone, but it depends on Castle Red for the King's flag and on Castle Black for its wood. The general form of the Initial and Entering Data Area is:

Initial and entering data area

    Raw initial data necessary for this submodel

    Data from another Submodel

    Data from yet another Submodel

While Step 3 continues to have complex data flows, it has established control over them by entering carefully. In every submodel, you can see that stone is quarried near Castle Yellow, and wood is lumbered near Castle Black. You know for sure where the design for each part of a castle comes from.

Because all exterior data enters a submodel at the top, references in the body of a submodel stay within the submodel or refer to the Initial and Entering Data Area. The data are visible locally if you wish to modify them locally. If Castle Yellow wanted to modify the "Red wall design," it would:

- Move the value from "From Castle Red" to "Initial Data," and

- Relabel the value "New wall design."

When data enter the submodel from other submodels, they should continue to be connected to the original source. An initial piece of data should exist in only one submodel's "raw initial data" area and be referred to by every other submodel in its "Entering from …" area (for example, the King's flag). If the entering piece of data comes from the body of another submodel, of course you point to the cell where it first appears. (In Castle Yellow's Initial and Entering Data Area, the red wall design points to Castle Red's wall.)

Because every formula in the body of a submodel goes through the Initial and Entering Data area on its way to the original source, the risk of intermediate error is introduced into the spreadsheet. Castle Black could mistakenly modify the design of the Yellow tower and not realize that it was no longer using the design from Castle Yellow. This risk of intermediate error is a high, but reasonable, price to pay for a clear division of the spreadsheet and a firm control of every submodel.

Submodel: The Reuse of Tools

Submodels provide you with a larger and more versatile library of tools to use in future models. Because the pieces are set up to become technically independent, you can use them in another context more quickly.

A user can "freeze" the numbers and labels in the Initial and Entering Data Area and cut the submodel out of the large model for independent use. A cut out submodel can be added to another model, connected where it needs to be and used with the conviction that it works.

With THREE CASTLE KINGDOM—Step 3 you can extract one submodel and use it on its own. An extracted Castle Yellow might look like this:

Strong

	A	B	C	D	E	F	G
1	Castle Yellow (extracted from THREE CASTLE KINGDOM—Step 3)						
2	Initial (and entering?) data						
3		Stone					
4		Yellow paint					
5		King's flag					
6		Red wall design					
7		Wood					
8		Black drawbridge design					
9	From ??						
10	From ??						
11	Model						
12		Yellow walls = red wall copy + stone + yellow paint					
13		Yellow tower = stone + yellow paint					
14		Yellow drawbridge = black drawbridge copy + wood + yellow paint					
15		Yellow castle = yellow walls + yellow drawbridge + yellow tower + King's flag					

In its independent form, all of Castle Yellow's Initial and Entering Data become Initial Data. Before Castle Yellow is successfully inserted in a new spreadsheet, data that come from submodels in the new spreadsheet would be broken out in "From ??" Areas.

A large model broken into submodels differs from a large integrated model because you can reassert full control over each submodel. First, you have intellectual control: Each model explains itself to the reader in a way the reader is likely to comprehend and remember. Second, you have physical control: If you want to temporarily exercise just one submodel you can do that by varying the values in the submodel's Initial and Entering Data Area. (This local variation may cut the submodel's ties to other submodels; the temporary version should be thrown away after use.) Third, you have evolutionary control: By breaking the model into pieces that correspond to business function (see the earlier discussion under the rule "Give a New Function a New Area") you give the future user a better chance to accurately modify the current spreadsheet to a future need. The model is more likely to evolve smoothly with the business it is intended to serve.

Below you see a family budget spreadsheet as it might evolve over time. The budget allows each member of the family to earn money. The family has fixed expenses that vary little from month to month. The family also has a few policies: The parents each get an allowance based on their monthly income, the father holds the family's entertainment budget, which is a percentage of the parent's joint earnings, the mother controls the clothing budget for the husband and son, the daughter may spend up to 33 percent of her earnings on clothes, the son must save 50 percent of his special earnings, and both children get a fixed allowance in addition to whatever they earn on their own.

Weak

	A	B	C	D	E	F	G	H
1	FAMLYFIN (Family Finance) 30 June 1600 B. Bunting							
2	(C) Copyright 1986 by John M. Nevison							
3								
4	Show the family's finances							
5								
6	Contents: (each section is a named range)							
7	INTRO		Introduction: Title, description, contents, and map					
8	INITIAL		Initial data and beginning assumptions					
9	MODEL		Model					
10	--							
11	Initial data and beginning assumptions							
12		5%	Percent of income permitted as parent allowance					
13		3%	Percent of joint parent income for entertainment					
14		33%	Percent of Daughter's earnings that may be spent on clothes					
15		50%	Percent of Son's earnings he must save					
16								
17			Springtime					
18		April	May	June				
19	Father							
20	Income	1000	900	1050				
21	House	450	450	450				
22	Fuel	200	0	0				
23	Insurance	0	0	250				
24	Mother							
25	Income	1000	1100	1200				
26	Health ins	300	300	300				
27	Car expenses	200	250	275				
28	Food	200	200	200				
29	Clothing	100	100	100				
30	Son							
31	Income	0	0	18				
32	Allowance	5	5	5				
33	Daughter							
34	Income	100	74	130				
35	Allowance	15	15	15				
36	--							

(continued)

	A	B	C	D	E	F	G	H
37	Model							
38			Springtime					
39		April	May	June	Total			
40	Father							
41	Income	1000	900	1050	2950			
42	House	450	450	450	1350			
43	Fuel	200	0	0	200			
44	Insurance	0	0	250	250			
45	Entertainment at %	60	60	68	188			
46	Allowance at %	50	45	53	148			
47								
48	Total family income	2100	2074	2398	6572			
49	Total family spending	1663	1504	1827	4994			
50	Total family saving	437	570	571	1578			
51								
52	Mother							
53	Income	1000	1100	1200	3300			
54	Health ins	300	300	300	900			
55	Car expenses	200	250	275	725			
56	Food	200	200	200	600			
57	Clothing	100	100	100	300			
58	Son	50	55	60	165			
59	Income	53	44	72	169			
60								
61	Son							
62	Income	0	0	18	18			
63	Allowance	5	5	5	15			
64	Extra spending	0	0	9	9			
65								
66	Daughter							
67	Income	100	74	130	304			
68	Allowance	15	15	15	45			
69	Clothing allowance	33	24	43	100			
70	===							

This model, while relatively small, has quite a few complex dependencies. The mother sums spending from the children and includes the teenage daughter's clothing allowance and the young son's extra spending. The father sums incomes from everyone, and expenses from the mother and himself.

The individual members of the family all wanted to have their own spreadsheets so they could control their own parts. The family agreed to split up the entertainment into equal parts, to divide the clothing allowance unevenly between the mother, father, and son, and establish individual submodels for each person.

Strong

	A	B	C	D	E	F	G	H
1	FAMILY (Family Individual Finance) 15 July 1600 B. Bunting							
2	(C) Copyright 1986 by John M. Nevison							
3								
4	Give each member of the family a submodel for each individual's budget.							
5								
6	Contents: (each section is a named range)							
7	INTRO		Introduction: Title, description, contents, and map					
8	INITIAL		Initial data and beginning assumptions					
9	SON		Son's submodel					
10	DAUGHTER		Daughter's submodel					
11	MOTHER		Mother's submodel					
12	FATHER		Father's submodel					
13	FAMILY		Family's summary submodel					
14	VERIFY		Verify area					
15	==							
16	Son's submodel							
17	SON'S INITIAL AND ENTERING DATA							
18		20%	Son's portion of clothing allowance					
19			(daughter excluded from allowance)					
20		50%	Percent of Son's earnings he must save					
21			Springtime					
22			April	May	June			
23	Outside income		0	0	18			
24	Allowance		5	5	5			
25	SON'S ENTERING DATA (FROM FATHER)							
26	Entertainment budget		15	15	17			
27	SON'S ENTERING DATA (FROM MOTHER)							
28	Clothing budget		100	100	100			
29	--							

(continued)

	A	B	C	D	E	F	G	H
30	SON'S BUDGET		Springtime					
31		April	May	June	Totals			
32	Outside income	0	0	18	18			
33	Spending							
34	Entertainment	15	15	17	47			
35	Allowance	5	5	5	15			
36	Clothing allowance	20	20	20	60			
37	Extra spending	0	0	9	9			
38	Total	40	40	51	131			
39								
40	Saving	0	0	9	9			
41	==							
42	Daughter's submodel							
43	DAUGHTER'S INITIAL AND ENTERING DATA							
44		33% Percent of Daughter's earnings that may be spent on clothes						
45			Springtime					
46		April	May	June				
47	Outside income	100	74	130				
48	Allowance	15	15	15				
49	DAUGHTER'S ENTERING DATA (FROM FATHER)							
50	Entertainment budget	15	15	17				
51	--							
52	DAUGHTER'S BUDGET		Springtime					
53		April	May	June	Totals			
54	Outside income	100	74	130	304			
55	Spending							
56	Entertainment	15	15	17	47			
57	Allowance	15	15	15	45			
58	Clothing allowance	33	24	43	100			
59	Total	63	54	75	192			
60								
61	Saving	67	50	87	204			
62	==							

(continued)

	A	B	C	D	E	F	G	H
63	Mother's submodel							
64	MOTHER'S INITIAL AND ENTERING DATA							
65		45% Mother's portion of clothing allowance						
66		5% Percent of income permitted as parent allowance						
67		Springtime						
68		April	May	June				
69	Outside income	1000	1100	1200				
70	Health ins	300	300	300				
71	Car expenses	200	250	275				
72	Food	200	200	200				
73	Family clothing budget	100	100	100				
74	MOTHER'S ENTERING DATA (FROM FATHER)							
75	Entertainment	15	15	17				
76	MOTHER'S ENTERING DATA (FROM SON)							
77	Total spending	40	40	51				
78	MOTHER'S ENTERING DATA (FROM DAUGHTER)							
79	Total spending	63	54	75				
80	---							
81	MOTHER'S BUDGET	Springtime						
82		April	May	June	Total			
83	Outside income	1000	1100	1200	3300			
84	Spending							
85	Health ins	300	300	300	900			
86	Car expenses	200	250	275	725			
87	Food	200	200	200	600			
88	Clothing allowance	45	45	45	135			
89	Allowance at %	50	55	60	165			
90	Entertainment	15	15	17	47			
91	Total	810	865	897	2572			
92								
93	Saving	190	235	303	728			
94	Other							
95	Children's spending	103	94	126	323			
96	===							

(continued)

	A	B	C	D	E	F	G	H
97	Father's submodel							
98	FATHER'S INITIAL AND ENTERING DATA							
99		35% Father's portion of clothing allowance						
100		3% Percent of joint parent income for entertainment						
101		4 Number of individuals sharing the entertainment budget						
102		5% Percent of income permitted as parent allowance						
103			Springtime					
104		April	May	June				
105	Outside income	1000	900	1050				
106	House	450	450	450				
107	Fuel	200	0	0				
108	Insurance	0	0	250				
109	FATHER'S ENTERING DATA (FROM MOTHER)							
110	Income	1000	1100	1200				
111	Clothing	100	100	100				
112	---							
113	FATHER'S BUDGET		Springtime					
114		April	May	June	Total			
115	Family entertainment	60	60	68	188			
116								
117	Outside income	1000	900	1050	2950			
118	Spending							
119	House	450	450	450	1350			
120	Fuel	200	0	0	200			
121	Insurance	0	0	250	250			
122	Allowance	50	45	53	148			
123	Entertainment	15	15	17	47			
124	Clothing allowance	35	35	35	105			
125	Total	750	545	804	2099			
126								
127	Saving	250	355	246	851			
128	===							

(continued)

	A	B	C	D	E	F	G	H
129	Family's summary submodel							
130			Springtime					
131		April	May	June				
132	FAMILY'S ENTERING DATA (FROM SON)							
133	Income	0	0	18				
134	Spending	40	40	51				
135	FAMILY'S ENTERING DATA (FROM DAUGHTER)							
136	Income	100	74	130				
137	Spending	63	54	75				
138	FAMILY'S ENTERING DATA (FROM MOTHER)							
139	Income	1000	1100	1200				
140	Spending	810	865	897				
141	FAMILY'S ENTERING DATA (FROM FATHER)							
142	Income	1000	900	1050				
143	Spending	750	545	804				
144	--							
145	FAMILY SUMMARY BUDGET	Springtime						
146		April	May	June	Total			
147	Total family income	2100	2074	2398	6572			
148	Total family spending	1663	1504	1827	4994			
149	Total family saving	437	570	571	1578			
150	==							
151	Verify Area							
152		3478.43	Model verification sum					
153								
154		18	Son's outside income total					
155		304	Daughter's outside income total					
156		728.125	Mother's total saving					
157		850.625	Father's total savings					
158		1577.68	Total family saving					
159	==							

While both of these examples basically do the same thing, the spreadsheet broken into submodels is clearly easier to use in pieces. The individual submodels allow each member of the family to control his or her own portion of the model. Note that whenever any one member corrects or changes his or her submodel, the other members of the family benefit from this change— everyone's submodel is revised to reflect the latest information.

The individual family members are here a metaphor for any organization that has divided its work into different, semi-autonomous tasks. Such tasks need to be handled a piece at a time. The corrections in one portion should be shared by all, and can be if each task is a submodel. The organization's results will be the integrated combination of all the pieces.

In the next strong example, any of NEWBUD's submodels could be broken out and turned over to the appropriate manager to work with. The president would get the executive budget; the vice president of manufacturing, the factory budget; the vice president of sales, the sales budget; the vice president of finance, the cash budget; the chairman of the board, the income statement and balance sheet. After they had each worked over their individual initial and entering data they could contribute their best estimate of their initial (but not entering) data to NEWBUD to see how the pieces fit together.

The Submodel Focuses Attention

Different tasks imply different focuses of attention. Even if one person is responsible for all the tasks in a spreadsheet, the submodel breakdown allows that individual to focus on one area at a time. This narrowing of focus increases understanding, speeds revision, and lowers the likelihood of introducing errors in a large model. (You only have to solve that portion of the problem you are interested in. You may leave the rest neatly alone and know that it is still okay.)

Such is not the case with a large integrated model—when you change one part, you must recheck it all to assure its integrity. Consider trying to understand the following model composed of six major parts. The basic idea is that four operating budgets (executive, factory, sales, and cash) coordinate with each other and then feed two accounting statements (the income statement and the balance sheet). (See Figure 5-2.)

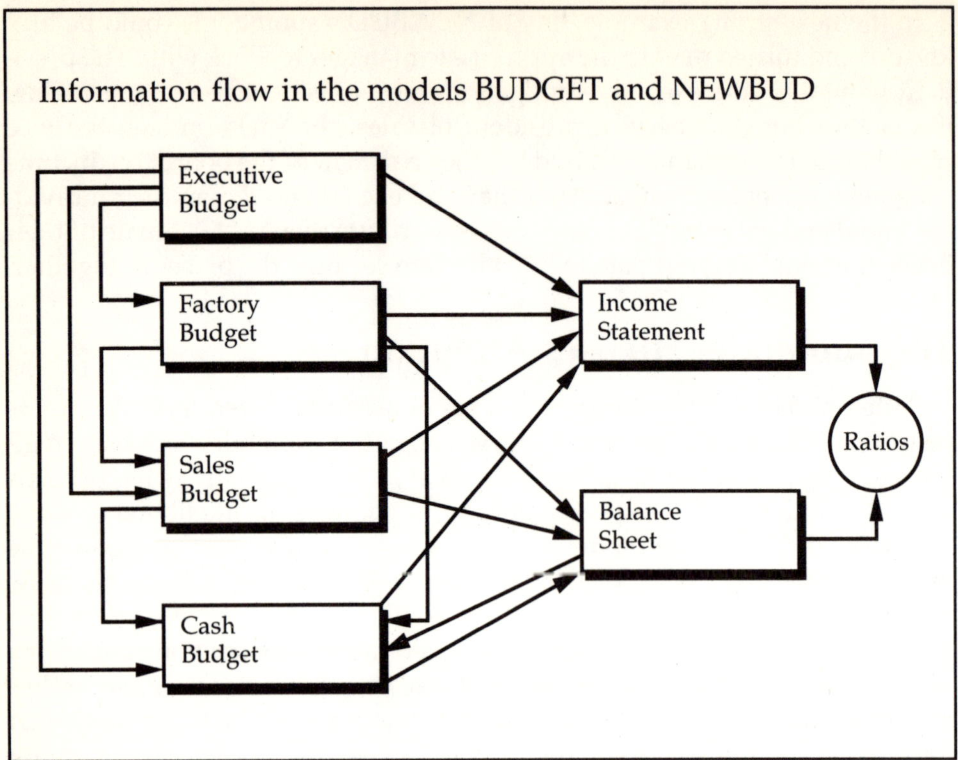

Figure 5-2. The complex information flows in the spreadsheets BUDGET and NEWBUD.

Contrast the terse, undocumented, large, complexly interrelated, and weak example called BUDGET with the same ideas broken up in manageable pieces in the strong example called NEWBUD. Ask yourself which example you would choose if your job required you to understand, use, and revise this model.

Weak

<table>
<tr><th></th><th>A</th><th>B</th><th>C</th><th>D</th><th>E</th><th>F</th><th>G</th><th>H</th></tr>
<tr><td>1</td><td colspan="8">BUDGET   1 January 1500   Peter Piper</td></tr>
<tr><td>2</td><td colspan="8"></td></tr>
<tr><td>3</td><td colspan="8">(C) Copyright 1983,1989 John M. Nevison</td></tr>
<tr><td>4</td><td colspan="8"></td></tr>
<tr><td>5</td><td colspan="8">Show how three operating budgets for executive office, factory,</td></tr>
<tr><td>6</td><td colspan="8">and sales office are combined to produce the operating</td></tr>
<tr><td>7</td><td colspan="8">cash budget and the annual accounting statements.</td></tr>
<tr><td>8</td><td colspan="8"></td></tr>
<tr><td>9</td><td colspan="8">Assumptions:</td></tr>
<tr><td>10</td><td></td><td></td><td>50%</td><td colspan="5">Percent exec. budget allocated to factory</td></tr>
<tr><td>11</td><td></td><td></td><td>50%</td><td colspan="5">Percent exec. budget allocated to sales</td></tr>
<tr><td>12</td><td></td><td></td><td>$0.20</td><td colspan="5">Mnfg labor $/unit</td></tr>
<tr><td>13</td><td></td><td></td><td>$0.37</td><td colspan="5">Raw material $/unit</td></tr>
<tr><td>14</td><td></td><td></td><td>45</td><td colspan="5">Average age of receivables (calendar days)</td></tr>
<tr><td>15</td><td></td><td></td><td>90</td><td colspan="5">Average age of payables (calendar days)</td></tr>
<tr><td>16</td><td></td><td></td><td>14.5%</td><td colspan="5">Annual interest rate</td></tr>
<tr><td>17</td><td></td><td></td><td>*</td><td colspan="5">Assumption somewhere in marked budget line</td></tr>
<tr><td>18</td><td colspan="8"></td></tr>
<tr><td>19</td><td></td><td>EXECUTIVE BUDGET</td><td>Qtr 1</td><td>Qtr 2</td><td>Qtr 3</td><td>Qtr 4</td><td>Year</td><td></td></tr>
<tr><td>20</td><td colspan="8"></td></tr>
<tr><td>21</td><td>*</td><td>Total</td><td>1,160</td><td>1,165</td><td>1,164</td><td>1,170</td><td>4,659</td><td></td></tr>
<tr><td>22</td><td colspan="8"></td></tr>
<tr><td>23</td><td colspan="8"></td></tr>
<tr><td>24</td><td colspan="8"></td></tr>
<tr><td>25</td><td></td><td>FACTORY DATA</td><td>Qtr 1</td><td>Qtr 2</td><td>Qtr 3</td><td>Qtr 4</td><td>Year</td><td></td></tr>
<tr><td>26</td><td colspan="8"></td></tr>
<tr><td>27</td><td>*</td><td>Units</td><td>22,361</td><td>22,600</td><td>22,500</td><td>22,600</td><td>90,061</td><td></td></tr>
<tr><td>28</td><td colspan="8"></td></tr>
<tr><td>29</td><td></td><td>FACTORY BUDGET</td><td></td><td></td><td></td><td></td><td></td><td></td></tr>
<tr><td>30</td><td colspan="8"></td></tr>
<tr><td>31</td><td></td><td>Direct costs</td><td></td><td></td><td></td><td></td><td></td><td></td></tr>
<tr><td>32</td><td></td><td>Mnfg labor</td><td>4,472</td><td>4,520</td><td>4,500</td><td>4,520</td><td>18,012</td><td></td></tr>
<tr><td>33</td><td></td><td>Raw materials</td><td>8,334</td><td>8,423</td><td>8,386</td><td>8,423</td><td>33,568</td><td></td></tr>
<tr><td>34</td><td>*</td><td>Power, heat, light</td><td>22</td><td>22</td><td>23</td><td>23</td><td>90</td><td></td></tr>
<tr><td>35</td><td></td><td>Total direct costs</td><td>12,829</td><td>12,965</td><td>12,909</td><td>12,966</td><td>51,670</td><td></td></tr>
<tr><td>36</td><td colspan="8"></td></tr>
<tr><td>37</td><td></td><td>Period costs</td><td></td><td></td><td></td><td></td><td></td><td></td></tr>
<tr><td>38</td><td>*</td><td>Supervision</td><td>310</td><td>325</td><td>365</td><td>300</td><td>1,300</td><td></td></tr>
<tr><td>39</td><td>*</td><td>Insurance</td><td>23</td><td>23</td><td>25</td><td>24</td><td>95</td><td></td></tr>
<tr><td>40</td><td>*</td><td>Depreciation</td><td>875</td><td>875</td><td>875</td><td>875</td><td>3,500</td><td></td></tr>
<tr><td>41</td><td>*</td><td>Management</td><td>1,800</td><td>1,850</td><td>1,900</td><td>1,780</td><td>7,330</td><td></td></tr>
<tr><td>42</td><td></td><td>Allocated corp. overhead</td><td>580</td><td>583</td><td>582</td><td>585</td><td>2,330</td><td></td></tr>
<tr><td>43</td><td></td><td>Total period costs</td><td>3,588</td><td>3,656</td><td>3,747</td><td>3,564</td><td>14,555</td><td></td></tr>
<tr><td>44</td><td colspan="8"></td></tr>
<tr><td>45</td><td></td><td>Total costs</td><td>16,417</td><td>16,621</td><td>16,656</td><td>16,530</td><td>66,224</td><td></td></tr>
</table>

(continued)

	A	B	C	D	E	F	G	H
46								
47								
48		SALES DATA	Qtr 1	Qtr 2	Qtr 3	Qtr 4	Year	
49								
50	*	Units	23,817	23,600	24,600	25,200	97,217	
51	*	Price	1.15	1.18	1.19	1.21		
52								
53		SALES BUDGET						
54								
55		Revenue	27,390	27,848	29,274	30,492	115,004	
56								
57		Factory costs	16,417	16,621	16,656	16,530	66,224	
58	*	Delivery	80	83	86	84	333	
59		Gross margin	10,893	11,144	12,532	13,878	48,446	
60								
61	*	Sales support	1,350	1,400	1,430	1,487	5,667	
62	*	Advertising	90	100	110	100	400	
63								
64	*	Selling and management	4,740	4,745	4,752	4,763	19,000	
65		Allocated corp. overhead	580	583	582	585	2,330	
66								
67		Contribution	20,550	20,938	22,314	23,473	87,274	
68								
69								
70		CASH BUDGET DATA						
71			Qtr 0	Qtr 1	Qtr 2	Qtr 3	Qtr 4	Year
72								
73	*	Units mfd	24,770	22,361	22,600	22,500	22,600	90,061
74	*	Units sold	23,000	23,817	23,600	24,600	25,200	97,217
75		Inventory change	1,770	-1,456	-1,000	-2,100	-2,600	-7,156
76	*	Sales on credit	24,150	27,390	27,848	29,274	30,492	115,004
77	*	Purchases on credit	8,424	8,334	8,423	8,386	8,423	33,568
78								
79		CASH BUDGET						
80								
81		Receipts	Qtr 0	Qtr 1	Qtr 2	Qtr 3	Qtr 4	Year
82		Collected receivables		25,770	27,619	28,561	29,883	111,833
83		Total receipts		25,770	27,619	28,561	29,883	111,833
84								

(continued)

	A	B	C	D	E	F	G	H
85		Disbursements						
86		Disbursed payables		8,424	8,334	8,423	8,386	33,568
87		Production payroll		4,472	4,520	4,500	4,520	18,012
88		Mnfing expenses		2,155	2,220	2,313	2,127	8,815
89		Selling expenses		6,260	6,328	6,378	6,434	25,400
90		Corp overhead		1,160	1,165	1,164	1,170	4,659
91		Interest		1,183	1,168	1,092	993	4,436
92	*	Taxes		1,200	1,300	1,450	1,650	5,600
93		Total disbursements		24,854	25,035	25,321	25,280	100,490
94								
95		Net cash		916	2,584	3,240	4,603	11,342
96								
97		Cumulative cash						
98		Beginning balance		32,000	32,500	33,000	33,500	32,000
99		Net cash		916	2,584	3,240	4,603	11,342
100	*	Minimum balance needed		500	500	500	500	2,000
101		Debt reduction (increase)		416	2,084	2,740	4,103	9,342
102		Ending balance	32,000	32,500	33,000	33,500	34,000	34,000
103		Debt	32,632	32,216	30,133	27,393	23,290	23,290
104								
105								
106								
107		ANNUAL STATEMENTS						
108								
109		INCOME STATEMENT	$					
110								
111		Sales	115,004					
112		Cost of goods	60,395					
113		Gross profit	54,608					
114								
115		Depreciation	3,500					
116		Selling genl. & admin.	30,059					
117								
118		Interest	4,436					
119								
120		Profit before taxes	16,613					
121		Tax	5,600					
122		Net income	11,013					
123								

(continued)

	A	B	C	D	E	F	G	H
124		BALANCE SHEET						
125			Last year	Change	This year			
126		Assets						
127								
128		Current assets						
129	*	Cash	32,000		34,000			
130		Accounts receivable	12,075		15,246			
131	*	Raw materials	2,500		2,500			
132	*	Finished goods	8,000	-4,098	3,902			
133		Total current assets	54,575		55,648			
134								
135		Fixed assets						
136	*	Land	2,222		2,222			
137	*	Plant and equipment	55,555		55,555			
138	*	Accumulated depreciation	11,111	3,500	14,611			
139		Net plant and equipment	44,444		40,944			
140		Total fixed assets	46,666		43,166			
141								
142	*	Other assets	999		999			
143								
144		Total assets	102,240		99,813			
145								
146		Liabilities and net worth						
147								
148		Current liabilities						
149		Accounts payable	8,424		8,423			
150	*	Notes payable	12,632	-9,342	3,290			
151		Total current liabilities	21,056		11,713			
152								
153	*	Long term liabilities	20,000		20,000			
154								
155		Common stock	35,629		40,544			
156	*	Retained earnings	25,555	2,000	27,555			
157								
158		Total liabilities and net worth	102,240		99,813			
159								
160								
161		RATIOS						
162								
163		Asset turnover	1.15					
164		Profit as a % of sales	9.6%					
165		Return on assets	11.0%					
166		Return on equity	16.2%					
167								

Strong

	A	B	C	D	E	F	G	H

```
 1  NEWBUD   2 January 1500   Peter Piper
 2                  20-Feb-89  : Date printed
 3  (C)Copyright 1985,1989 John M. Nevison
 4
 5  Combine three operating budgets for executive office, factory,
 6  and sales office to produce the operating cash budget,
 7  the income statement, and the balance sheet.
 8
 9  This spreadsheet illustrates a cooperating network of models.
10
11  For a detailed explanation of the model see Chapter Two of the
12  following reference:
13          Nevison, John M., "Executive Computing: How to Get It Done
14          With Spreadsheets and Graphs," Atlanta: GA, Association for
15          Media-Based Continuing Education for Engineers, 1986.
16
17  Contents (Each area is a named range):
18
19      INTRODUCTION            Title, intro., contents, and references
20      VERIFY                  Verify area
21      EXECUTIVE               Executive Office Budget (and initial data)
22      FACTORY                 Factory Budget (and initial data)
23      SALES                   Sales Budget (and initial data)
24      CASH                    Cash Budget (and initial data)
25      INCOME                  Income Statement (and initial data)
26      BALANCE                 Balance Sheet (and initial data)
27      RATIOS                  Financial Ratios (report)
28  -----------------------------------------------------------------------
29  Verify area
30                  232,732  Verification sum
31
32  If an error appears here, check below and then the appropriate area of the model.
33  (Be sure you have recalculated the whole model.)
34
35               66,224  Factory budget, total yearly costs
36               21,050  Sales budget, total yearly contribution
37               11,342  Cash budget, yearly net cash
38               23,290  Cash budget, end of year debt
39               11,014  Income statement, net income
40               99,813  Balance sheet, this year's total liabilities
41                       and net worth
42  =======================================================================
```

(continued)

	A	B	C	D	E	F	G	H
43	EXECUTIVE BUDGET INITIAL DATA							
44		Qtr 1	Qtr 2	Qtr 3	Qtr 4			
45	Totals	1,160	1,165	1,164	1,170			
46	---							
47	EXECUTIVE BUDGET							
48		Qtr 1	Qtr 2	Qtr 3	Qtr 4	Year		
49	Total	1,160	1,165	1,164	1,170	4,659		
50	===							
51	FACTORY BUDGET INITIAL DATA							
52		50%	Percent exec. budget allocated to factory					
53		$0.20	Mnfg labor $/unit					
54		$0.37	Raw material $/unit					
55		Qtr 1	Qtr 2	Qtr 3	Qtr 4			
56	Units mfd	22,361	22,600	22,500	22,600			
57	Power, heat, light	22	22	23	23			
58	Supervision	310	325	365	300			
59	Insurance	23	23	25	24			
60	Depreciation	875	875	875	875			
61	Management	1,800	1,850	1,900	1,780			
62								
63	FACTORY BUDGET ASSUMPTIONS (From executive budget)							
64	Total executive budget	1,160	1,165	1,164	1,170			
65	---							
66	FACTORY BUDGET							
67		Qtr 1	Qtr 2	Qtr 3	Qtr 4	Year		
68	Direct costs							
69	Mnfg labor	4,472	4,520	4,500	4,520	18,012		
70	Raw materials	8,334	8,423	8,386	8,423	33,568		
71	Power, heat, light	22	22	23	23	90		
72	Total direct costs	12,829	12,965	12,909	12,966	51,670		
73								
74	Period costs							
75	Supervision	310	325	365	300	1,300		
76	Insurance	23	23	25	24	95		
77	Depreciation	875	875	875	875	3,500		
78	Management	1,800	1,850	1,900	1,780	7,330		
79	Allocated corp. overhead	580	583	582	585	2,330		
80	Total period costs	3,588	3,656	3,747	3,564	14,555		
81								
82	Total costs	16,417	16,621	16,656	16,530	66,224		
83	===							

(continued)

	A	B	C	D	E	F	G	H
84	SALES DATA INITIAL DATA							
85	50% Percent exec. budget allocated to sales							
86		Qtr 1	Qtr 2	Qtr 3	Qtr 4			
87	Units sold	23,817	23,600	24,600	25,200			
88	Price	1	1	1	1			
89	Delivery	80	83	86	84			
90	Sales support	1,350	1,400	1,430	1,487			
91	Advertising	90	100	110	100			
92	Selling and management	4,740	4,745	4,752	4,763			
93								
94	SALES DATA ASSUMPTIONS (From executive budget)							
95	Total executive budget	1,160	1,165	1,164	1,170			
96								
97	SALES DATA ASSUMPTIONS (From factory budget)							
98	Total factory costs	16,417	16,621	16,656	16,530			
99	--------							
100	SALES BUDGET	Qtr 1	Qtr 2	Qtr 3	Qtr 4	Year		
101								
102	Revenue	27,390	27,848	29,274	30,492	115,004		
103								
104	Factory costs	16,417	16,621	16,656	16,530	66,224		
105	Delivery	80	83	86	84	333		
106	Gross margin	10,893	11,144	12,532	13,878	48,446		
107								
108	Sales support	1,350	1,400	1,430	1,487	5,667		
109	Advertising	90	100	110	100	400		
110								
111	Selling and management	4,740	4,745	4,752	4,763	19,000		
112	Allocated corp. overhead	580	583	582	585	2,330		
113								
114	Contribution	4,133	4,317	5,658	6,943	21,050		
115	=========							
116	CASH BUDGET INITIAL DATA							
117	45 Average age of receivables (calendar days)							
118	90 Average age of payables (calendar days)							
119	14.5% Annual interest rate							
120		Qtr 0	Qtr 1	Qtr 2	Qtr 3	Qtr 4		
121	Units mfd	24,770						
122	Units sold	23,000						
123	Sales on credit	24,150						
124	Purchases on credit	8,424						
125	Taxes		1,200	1,300	1,450	1,650		
126	Minimum balance needed		500	500	500	500		
127								

(continued)

	A	B	C	D	E	F	G	H
128	CASH BUDGET ASSUMPTIONS (from exec. budget)							
129	Total exec. budget		1,160	1,165	1,164	1,170		
130								
131	CASH BUDGET ASSUMPTIONS (from factory budget)							
132			Qtr 1	Qtr 2	Qtr 3	Qtr 4		
133	Units mfd		22,361	22,600	22,500	22,600		
134	Purchases on credit		8,334	8,423	8,386	8,423		
135	Mnfg labor		4,472	4,520	4,500	4,520		
136	Power, heat, light		22	22	23	23		
137	Supervision		310	325	365	300		
138	Insurance		23	23	25	24		
139	Management		1,800	1,850	1,900	1,780		
140								
141	CASH BUDGET ASSUMPTIONS (from sales budget)							
142	Units sold		23,817	23,600	24,600	25,200		
143	Sales on credit		27,390	27,848	29,274	30,492		
144	Delivery		80	83	86	84		
145	Sales support		1,350	1,400	1,430	1,487		
146	Advertising		90	100	110	100		
147	Selling and management		4,740	4,745	4,752	4,763		
148								
149	CASH BUDGET ASSUMPTIONS (from last year's balance sheet)							
150	Cash	32,000						
151	Notes payable	12,632						
152	Long term liabilities	20,000						
153	---							
154	CASH BUDGET							
155	Tricky formulas:							
156	Collected receivables =		(Avg age of rec./90) * last qtr sales +					
157			(90 - Avg age of rec.)/90 * curr qtr sales					
158	Dispersed payables =		(Avg age of pay./90) * last qtr sales +					
159			(90 - Avg age of pay.)/90 * curr qtr sales					
160	Mnfg expenses = Power heat and light + supervision + insurance + management							
161	Selling expenses = Delivery + sales support + advertising + selling and mgt							
162	Interest = Annual int rate/4 * prior qtr's debt							
163	Cash ending balance = Beginning balance + net cash - debt reduction							
164	Debt = Prior qtr's debt - debt reduction							
165								
166		Qtr 0	Qtr 1	Qtr 2	Qtr 3	Qtr 4	Year	
167	Inventory change—units	1,770	-1,456	-1,000	-2,100	-2,600	-7,156	
168								
169	Receipts							
170	Collected receivables		25,770	27,619	28,561	29,883	111,833	
171	Total receipts		25,770	27,619	28,561	29,883	111,833	
172								

(continued)

	A	B	C	D	E	F	G	H
173	Disbursements							
174	Disbursed payables		8,424	8,334	8,423	8,386	33,568	
175	Production payroll		4,472	4,520	4,500	4,520	18,012	
176	Mnfg expenses		2,155	2,220	2,313	2,127	8,815	
177	Selling expenses		6,260	6,328	6,378	6,434	25,400	
178	Corp. overhead		1,160	1,165	1,164	1,170	4,659	
179	Interest		1,183	1,168	1,092	993	4,436	
180	Taxes		1,200	1,300	1,450	1,650	5,600	
181	Total disbursements		24,854	25,035	25,321	25,280	100,490	
182								
183	Net cash		916	2,584	3,240	4,603	11,342	
184								
185	Cumulative cash							
186	Beginning balance		32,000	32,500	33,000	33,500	32,000	
187	Net cash		916	2,584	3,240	4,603	11,342	
188	Minimum balance needed		500	500	500	500	2,000	
189	Debt reduction (increase)		416	2,084	2,740	4,103	9,342	
190	Ending balance	32,000	32,500	33,000	33,500	34,000	34,000	
191	Debt	32,632	32,216	30,133	27,393	23,290	23,290	
192	===							
193	INCOME STATEMENT ASSUMPTIONS (from exec. budget)							
194	4,659 Total executive budget (corporate overhead)							
195								
196	INCOME STATEMENT ASSUMPTIONS (from factory budget)							
197	3,500 Total depreciation							
198	2,330 Total corp overhead allocated							
199	66,224 Total costs							
200								
201	INCOME STATEMENT ASSUMPTIONS (from sales budget)							
202	115,004 Total revenue							
203	333 Total delivery costs							
204	5,667 Total sales support costs							
205	400 Total advertising costs							
206	19,000 Total selling and management costs							
207								
208	INCOME STATEMENT ASSUMPTIONS (from cash budget)							
209	4,436 Total interest							
210	5,600 Total tax							
211	---							

(continued)

	A	B	C	D	E	F	G	H
212	INCOME STATEMENT							
213	Tricky formulas:							
214	Cost of goods sold = Factory budget costs (less depreciation and corporate overhead)							
215	Selling, general and administrative = All the sales budget costs and the executive budget							
216		$	% of Sales					
217	Sales	115,004	100%					
218	Cost of goods	60,395	53%					
219	Gross profit	54,609	47%					
220								
221	Depreciation	3,500	3%					
222	Selling genl. & admin.	30,059	26%					
223								
224	Interest	4,436	4%					
225								
226	Profit before taxes	16,614	14%					
227	Tax	5,600	5%					
228	Net income	11,014	10%					
229	===							
230	BALANCE SHEET INITIAL DATA							
231		Last year						
232		32,000	Cash					
233		2,500	Raw materials					
234		8,000	Finished goods					
235		2,222	Land					
236		55,555	Plant and equipment					
237		11,111	Accumulated depreciation					
238		999	Other assets					
239		12,632	Notes payable					
240		20,000	Long term liabilities					
241		25,555	Retained earnings					
242								
243		2,000	Increase (decrease) in retained earnings last					
244			year to this year					
245								
246	BALANCE SHEET ASSUMPTIONS (from factory budget)							
247		$0.20	Mnfg labor $/unit					
248		$0.37	Raw material $/unit					
249		8,423	Qtr 4 raw material (purchases on credit)					
250		3,500	Total depreciation					
251								
252	BALANCE SHEET ASSUMPTIONS (from sales budget)							
253		30,492	Qtr 4 revenue (sales on credit)					
254								

(continued)

	A	B	C	D	E	F	G	H
255	BALANCE SHEET ASSUMPTIONS (from cash budget)							
256		45	Average age of receivables (calendar days)					
257		90	Average age of payables (calendar days)					
258		8,424	Qtr 0 raw material (purchases on credit)					
259		24,150	Qtr 0 revenue (sales on credit)					
260		-7,156	Total inventory change—units					
261		9,342	Debt reduction (increase)					
262		34,000	Ending balance of cumulative cash					
263	---							
264	BALANCE SHEET							
265	Tricky formulas:							
266	Cash (this year) = from accumulated cash budget							
267	Accounts receivable = Average age of receivables/90 * 0th or 4th qtr sales on credit							
268	Change in finished goods = change in inventory units from cash budget *							
269	(raw mat cost/unit + mfg labor cost/unit)							
270	Change in depreciation = from factory budget							
271	Accounts payable = Average age of payables/90 * 0th or 4th qtr purchases on credit							
272	Change in notes payable = from cash budget debt reduction							
273	Change in retained earnings = from assumptions							
274	Common stock (this year) = Total assets - short and long term liabilities - retained earnings							
275								
276		BALANCE SHEET						
277	Assets	Last year	Change	This year				
278								
279	Current assets							
280	Cash	32,000		34,000				
281	Accounts receivable	12,075		15,246				
282	Raw materials	2,500		2,500				
283	Finished goods	8,000	-4,098	3,902				
284	Total current assets	54,575		55,648				
285								
286	Fixed assets							
287	Land	2,222		2,222				
288	Plant and equipment	55,555		55,555				
289	Accumulated depreciation	11,111	3,500	14,611				
290	Net plant and equipment	44,444		40,944				
291	Total fixed assets	46,666		43,166				
292								
293	Other assets	999		999				
294								
295	Total assets	102,240		99,813				
296								

(continued)

	A	B	C	D	E	F	G	H
297	Liabilities and net worth							
298								
299	Current liabilities							
300	Accounts payable	8,424		8,423				
301	Notes payable	12,632	-9,342	3,290				
302	Total current liabilities	21,056		11,713				
303								
304	Long term liabilities	20,000		20,000				
305								
306	Common stock	35,629		40,544				
307	Retained earnings	25,555	2,000	27,555				
308								
309	Total liabilities and net worth	102,240		99,813				
310	==							
311	RATIOS ASSUMPTIONS FROM INCOME STATEMENT							
312	115,004 Sales							
313	11,014 Net income							
314	RATIOS ASSUMPTIONS FROM BALANCE SHEET							
315	99,813 Total assets							
316	40,544 Common stock							
317	27,555 Retained earnings							
318	---							
319	RATIOS (Report from income statement and balance sheet)							
320	20-Jan-91							
321	Corporate Financial Ratios			Formula is:				
322								
323	Asset turnover	1.15		Sales/total assets				
324	Profit as a % of sales	9.6%		Net income/Sales				
325	Return on assets	11.0%		Net income/total assets				
326	Return on equity	16.2%		Net income/				
327				(Common stock + retained earnings)				
328	==							

The strong version of this model, NEWBUD, gives you, the reader, much more to work with. If you ever really wanted to understand what was going on in this model, you would study NEWBUD, not BUDGET. NEWBUD's biggest distinction is that it gives you a chance to learn one section at a time. You can understand and use one section without having mastered all of the other sections. Submodels give you intellectual control. NEWBUD also provides a Verify Area so you have the reassurance that all the submodels are operating correctly.

Collections of Spreadsheets

The cooperative effort, shown here on one spreadsheet, is also possible among several spreadsheets. The same Initial and Entering Data Area makes possible the coordinated use of several sheets. As the number of spreadsheets grows, the need for organization and documentation grows faster. When several spreadsheets are involved, you need a piece of paper with a picture of the whole system and directions on how to use your portion of it. To the greatest extent possible, you should include the documentation in the cooperating models themselves. (These issues will be discussed further in the Chapter 6.)

1-2-3 Release 3 makes the use of submodels even more appealing because each submodel can begin on a new page. If your large spreadsheets are broken up into groups of pages that correspond to submodels, you will be able to develop a tool kit of submodels that you can use in several models. The overall documentation of each model should be done in the Introduction Area on the first page.

So when your work group has a team activity where the division of labor dictates that each member knows part of the data best, you may find that the helpful spreadsheet is really a collection of submodels. Each member of the team can use his or her submodel secure in the knowledge that the pieces will work together because each submodel always makes sure that its data enters carefully.

6

Two Worked Examples

PAIRS OR PEARS
Twelve pairs hanging high,
Twelve knights riding by,
Each knight took a pear,
And yet left a dozen there.

The proof of the rules is in their use. The first question to answer is "How do the rules feel when you use them to build a new spreadsheet?" The second question is "How do the rules feel when you use them to modify an old spreadsheet?" To see how the rules work in practice, we will work through two examples, one from initial idea to final spreadsheet and one from slightly styled to fully restyled. We will make notes as we go, trying to see how the rules feel in practice, how long things really take to do, and how the rules can speed the development of a structured spreadsheet.

Building a New Spreadsheet: PROGRESS

The beginning of this spreadsheet is the template FULL RULE. We choose this template because it contains all the rules and we want them to remind us to do the right thing.

The first thing we need is a temporary name for this model. What we want to do is develop a model that contains a practical layout of a departmental budget, so we decide to call this model DEPARTMENT. We save a copy of the template under this new name.

Department   23 October 1986   John M. Nevison

After the new name we say out loud what we have only half thought out—"The purpose of this model is…". We write down our answer and stare at the result for a few minutes, decide that it is a full order, but reasonable at this stage. We correct the spelling errors and erase the rules TITLE TO TELL (this title could probably be improved; let's keep alert to that possibility as we work), MAKE A FORMAL INTRODUCTION (that's ensured by the structure of the introduction area in the template), and DECLARE THE MODEL'S PURPOSE (just finished doing the first draft of that).

The purpose of this model is to illustrate a well made spreadsheet that provides a department manager with the tools he needs to manage his departmental budget. In particular:

A 12 month plan for the year
A month-by-month list of the actual expenses as they occur
Reports and graphs for the manager
Reports and graphs to be posted for the department to see
Reports and graphs for upper management

This statement of purpose begs the issue of what the reports and graphs actually are, but does alert us to the necessity of getting a clear picture of what they should be before we invest a great deal of time entering data into this model. We decide to begin with a simple list of reports in the Report Area and graphs in the Graph Area. We hope that if we choose explicit titles for these reports, we can then sketch them on a piece of paper or sketch them into the spreadsheet. If we know what some (not necessarily all) of the results are, we can then work back to the initial data and be reasonably sure that we won't forget a major item. We design backward, from desired results to necessary initial conditions.

Report Area
          REPORT TO YOUR READER
Departmental Quarterly goals—public
Departmental Totals. Sales, Costs, Profits budget versus Actual—public
Departmental Detailed costs, Budgeted versus Actual—Dept. manager
Sales and selling costs—Dept. manager
Departmental YTD Profit Performance, Budgeted, Actual, Forecast—upper
    management

Graph Area
          GRAPH TO ILLUMINATE
Departmental Quarterly Sales Goal progress-to-date line chart—public
Departmental Totals. Sales, Costs, Profits Budgeted versus Actual—YTD each
    month bar chart
Sales and selling costs —Dept. manager
Departmental YTD Profit Performance, Budgeted, Actual, Forecast—line chart on
    profit

The intended reader is included with the title of the reports and graphs in order to sharpen the focus of what should be included. The effect of this list is that we feel we can go off and rough out some reports and sketch some graphs. At this point we're beginning to feel some discomfort because we want to have fun with the spreadsheet model itself. Our better half, how-ever, tells us first to refine what we think we want in each report and graph. (FIRST DESIGN ON PAPER.)

The results of the reports take longer than we thought they would (about three hours). We find that we spend a great deal of time thinking through the best way to REPORT TO YOUR READER. We vary column widths. We change and rearrange rows (and columns). We format the column headings to the right side of the cells. We format the pseudonumbers and ask and re-ask if the current report is the best one for the reader. We quit working on the reports when we feel that we must know more about the actual values of the numbers to improve our thinking about the report formats.

	A	B	C	D	E	F	G
214	Department goals for the quarter						
215		OUR DEPARTMENT'S QUARTERLY PERFORMANCE					
216		FOR MONTH OF MAY (Month 2 of Quarter 2)					
217		Actual	Qtrly goal	Miles to go	Rate so far	Comment	
218	Sales	xxx.xxx	xxx.xxx	xxx.xxx	xx%	The the the	
219	Costs	xxx.xxx	xxx.xxx	xxx.xxx	xx%	The the the	
220	Profits	xxx.xxx	xxx.xxx	xxx.xxx	xx%	The the the	
221	--						
222	Department's year-to-date performance						
223		OUR DEPARTMENT'S YEAR-TO-DATE PERFORMANCE					
224		FOR MONTH OF MAY (Month 5 of 12)					
225		Actual	Budgeted	Rate so far	Forecast *	Rate so far	Remaining
226	Sales	xxx.xxx	xxx.xxx	xx%	xxx.xxx	xx%	xxx.xxx
227	Costs	xxx.xxx	xxx.xxx	xx%	xxx.xxx	xx%	xxx.xxx
228	Profits	xxx.xxx	xxx.xxx	xx%	xxx.xxx	xx%	xxx.xxx
229		*Forecast is Revison of Budget					
230	--						
231	Department cost analysis						
232	DEPARTMENTAL COST ANALYSIS						
233		FOR MONTH OF MAY (Month 2 of Quarter 2)					
234		Month	Budget/for	Difference	Qtr	Budget/for	Difference
235	Item	xxx.xxx	xxx.xxx	xxx.xxx	xxx.xxx	xxx.xxx	xxx.xxx
236	Item	xxx.xxx	xxx.xxx	xxx.xxx	xxx.xxx	xxx.xxx	xxx.xxx
237	Item	xxx.xxx	xxx.xxx	xxx.xxx	xxx.xxx	xxx.xxx	xxx.xxx
238	Item	xxx.xxx	xxx.xxx	xxx.xxx	xxx.xxx	xxx.xxx	xxx.xxx
239	Item	xxx.xxx	xxx.xxx	xxx.xxx	xxx.xxx	xxx.xxx	xxx.xxx
240							
241	Total	xxx.xxx	xxx.xxx	xxx.xxx	xxx.xxx	xxx.xxx	xxx.xxx
242	--						
243	Sales and selling costs						
244		SALES AND SELLING COSTS					
245		January	February	March	April	May	June
246	Sales	xxx.xxx	xxx.xxx	xxx.xxx	xxx.xxx	xxx.xxx	xxx.xxx
247	Costs	xxx.xxx	xxx.xxx	xxx.xxx	xxx.xxx	xxx.xxx	xxx.xxx
248	% of sales	xx%	xx%	xx%	xx%	xx%	xx%
249	Smoothed(5 mth)						
250	% of sales	xx%	xx%	xx%	xx%	xx%	xx%
251	--						
252	Department profit performance						
253	IDEAL DEPARTMENT YEAR-TO-DATE PROFIT PERFORMANCE						
254	12-Jun-86	YTD	YTD		Annual	Annual	
255		Budget	Actual	Rate	Budget	Forecast	cast/Budget
256	Sales	xxx.xxx	xxx.xxx	xx%	xxx.xxx	xxx.xxx	xx%
257	Variable costs	xxx.xxx	xxx.xxx	xx%	xxx.xxx	xxx.xxx	xx%
258	Fixed costs	xxx.xxx	xxx.xxx	xx%	xxx.xxx	xxx.xxx	xx%
259							
260	Profit	xxx.xxx	xxx.xxx	xx%	xxx.xxx	xxx.xxx	xx%
261	--						

The worst thing about these reports is that we know that we may change their format later. We have, however, achieved what we came for: a sharpened sense of exactly what data we will need and what the main model will look like.

To be sure we know what the results look like on paper, we print a full copy of the reports. (TEST THE MODEL—PRACTICE AND PROOFREAD.) The printed versions reveal a few minor items that we want to add, but basically confirm that these are the desired reports.

After finishing the review of the paper copy of the reports, we sketch on paper what the graphs might look like and capture the outcome of that work with some notes in the Graph Area.

	A	B	C	D	E	F	G	H
262	Graph area							
263			GRAPH TO ILLUMINATE					
264	Departmental Quarterly Goals:Sales, Costs, Profits. Public three pairs of bar charts.							
265	Sales and selling costs. Rough and smooth line chart. Last several years and last 12 months.							
266	Departmental Profit Performance, Budgeted, Actual, Current Forecast—line							
267	chart on profits—upper management							
268	---							

What we learn is that we need fewer graphs than we had thought. The selling efficiency graph, however, will require more data than only the current year: It will require 13 months of back data.

Now a first draft of the outcomes of the spreadsheet has been completed. (Note that we have ambitions of serving several constituencies with one spreadsheet because we know one model can spawn several reports with several Report Areas.) We are ready to go back to the basic model and the departmental data we need to feed the model. Elapsed time at this point is four hours.

In the model itself we decide we want to see several measures at once: Monthly, quarterly, half-year, and yearly. These measures will allow the department manager to pick and choose good features for quick reports on the department's performance. (If the quarterly performance is poor, the six-month figures can be emphasized.)

After an hour or so of varying the structure we decide that we will define the "plan" to be the original budget plus periodic reforecasts to year end. Plan is the best current guess at anticipated performance. In the present case, with only one reforecast made in June, the plan is the January–May Budget and the June–December Forecast. If a second reforecast were made in September, the plan would have three legs: January–May, June–September, and

October–December. Because the manager will want to see how close performance is to anticipated performance, the six areas necessary are:

Monthly plan
Monthly actual
Monthly difference
Summary plan
Summary actual
Summary difference

With these six sections, the manager can illustrate in a few pages how the business performs. The manager can wait a few days for the spreadsheet operator to adjust the Report Areas to generate the proper month's reports and graphs.

Next we turn to the Initial Data Area to enter the data necessary to make the model real. We begin with the historical sales data because we know the model will need it to do one of the desired graphs. Then we put in the budget, the actuals to date, and the plan (which is composed of original budget numbers and later forecasts for the remainder of the year).

	A	B	C	D	E	F	G	H	I	J	K
57	Initial data and beginning assumptions										
58		May :Current month									
59											
60	BACK DATA	Jan.	Feb.	Mar.	Apr.	May	Jun.	Jul.	Aug.	Sep.	Oct.
61	Sales 84	12	17	19	23	22	19	18	15	18	20
62	Sales 85	15	17	21	27	25	20	19	14	20	22
63	Cost of selling 84	5.5	5.5	5.5	6.0	6.0	6.0	5.5	5.5	5.5	5.5
64	Cost of selling 85	5.5	5.5	5.5	5.5	5.5	5.5	5.5	5.5	5.5	5.5
65											
66	ORIG. BUDGET	Jan.	Feb.	Mar.	Apr.	May	Jun.	Jul.	Aug.	Sep.	Oct.
67	Sales	16.0	19.0	23.0	30.0	28.0	22.0	21.0	15.0	22.0	24.0
68	Delivery costs	0.5	0.6	0.7	0.9	0.8	0.6	0.4	0.4	0.7	0.7
69	Raw material	2.4	2.8	3.4	4.5	4.2	3.3	3.0	2.2	3.3	3.6
70	Mfg costs	1.9	2.3	2.8	3.6	3.4	2.6	2.5	1.8	2.6	2.9
71	Cost of selling	5.5	5.5	5.5	6.0	6.0	5.5	5.5	5.5	5.5	5.5
72	Plant costs	1.0	1.0	1.0	1.0	1.0	1.0	1.0	1.0	1.0	1.0
73	Office costs	0.6	0.6	0.6	0.6	0.6	0.6	0.6	0.6	0.6	0.6
74	Admin. salaries	4.0	4.0	4.0	4.0	4.0	4.0	4.0	4.0	4.0	4.0
75	Profit	0.1	2.2	5	9.4	8	4.4	4	-0.5	4.3	5.7
76											

(continued)

	A	B	C	D	E	F	G	H
118	Margin	33%	33%	33%	33%	33%	33%	33%
119	Annual Sales	44,550	47,052	54,354	60,931	64,980	70,491	77,302
120	Cum cash	11,880	14,233	21,548	32,648	47,100	64,934	86,496
121	Firm C							
122	Mkt share	33%	29%	24%	19%	17%	17%	17%
123	Annual units	2,970	3,654	4,234	4,357	4,678	5,614	6,737
124	Annual debt	32,670	27,256	12,744	(6,846)	(25,764)	(35,909)	(42,241)
125	Cum volume	2,970	6,624	10,858	15,215	19,893	25,507	32,243
126	Cost/unit	$10.03	$7.75	$6.61	$5.93	$5.44	$5.02	$4.66
127	Price	$15.00	$13.27	$11.28	$10.17	$8.00	$6.47	$5.91
128	Margin	33%	42%	41%	42%	32%	22%	21%
129	Annual Sales	44,550	48,477	47,766	44,313	37,413	36,314	39,822
130	Cum cash	11,880	21,221	35,022	51,159	63,177	72,222	82,063
131	---							
132	Report area							

	A	B	C	D		F	G	H
133	Year	1				10		
134	Annual Market	12,600				82,170		
135	Cum Market	21,600				417,597		
136	Avg Price/unit	$11.32				$4.36		
137								
138	Firms	A	B	C		A	B	C
139	Mkt share	38%	33%	29%		50%	33%	17%
140								
141	Annual units	4,788	4,158	3,654		41,085	27,116	13,969
142	Annual debt	39,771	32,818	27,256		(190,126)	(103,859)	(71,719)
143	(surplus)							
144	Cum volume	7,758	7,128	6,624		204,063	137,807	75,637
145	Cost/unit	$7.36	$7.57	$7.75		$2.57	$2.92	$3.54
146								
147	Price	$9.83	$11.32	$13.27		$4.36	$4.36	$4.36
148								
149	Margin	25%	33%	42%		41%	33%	19%
150								
151	Annual Sales	47,052	47,052	48,477		179,174	118,255	60,919
152								
153	Cum cash	7,281	14,233	21,221		369,299	222,114	132,638
154	---							

(continued)

	A	B	C	D	E	F	G	H
155	Graph area							
156	1. "Firm pricing" — three firms in the market							
157	2. "Market share" — three firms market share over 10 years							
158	3. "Cumulative cash" — three firms 10 year net cash							
159			Price				Log(price)	
160		Year	Price A	Price B	Price C	Firm A	Firm B	Firm C
161		0	15.00	15.00	15.00	1.18	1.18	1.18
162		1	9.83	11.32	13.27	0.99	1.05	1.12
163		2	8.25	9.34	11.28	0.92	0.97	1.05
164		3	7.21	8.05	10.17	0.86	0.91	1.01
165		4	6.87	7.16	8.00	0.84	0.85	0.90
166		5	6.47	6.47	6.47	0.81	0.81	0.81
167		6	5.91	5.91	5.91	0.77	0.77	0.77
168		7	5.44	5.44	5.44	0.74	0.74	0.74
169		8	5.04	5.04	5.04	0.70	0.70	0.70
170		9	4.68	4.68	4.68	0.67	0.67	0.67
171		10	4.36	4.36	4.36	0.64	0.64	0.64
172								
173			Market share			Cumulative cash ($1000)		
174		Year	A	B	C	A	B	C
175		0	0.33	0.33	0.33	12	12	12
176		1	0.38	0.33	0.29	7	14	21
177		2	0.43	0.33	0.24	9	22	35
178		3	0.48	0.33	0.19	18	33	51
179		4	0.50	0.33	0.17	39	47	63
180		5	0.50	0.33	0.17	71	65	72
181		6	0.50	0.33	0.17	110	86	82
182		7	0.50	0.33	0.17	159	112	93
183		8	0.50	0.33	0.17	217	143	105
184		9	0.50	0.33	0.17	286	179	118
185		10	0.50	0.33	0.17	369	222	133
186	--							
187	Verify area							
188	550244.68 Verification sum							
189	If an error appears here, check below and the appropriate area of the							
190	spreadsheet. (Be sure that you have recalculated the whole model.)							
191	10.00 Initial data's market share years 2–10 sum of checksums							
192	417597.01 Model's year 10 cumulative market							
193	132637.67 Report Year 10 Firm C's cumulative cash							
194	===							

An Afterword on Experience Curve Mathematics

An experience curve such as the one in Figure 6-1 is a function of the cumulative volume that yields the current unit cost. The unit cost is calculated from the startup unit cost, the cumulative volume, the startup volume, and the experience curve "slope." When the cumulative volume doubles, the unit cost drops to a fixed percentage, say 80 percent, of its prior value. For example, if your initial startup unit cost was $100 and your startup volume was 1,000 units, when you reach 2,000 units the unit cost will be $80, and when you reach 4,000 units the cost will be $64. The 80 percent is called the "slope" of the experience curve.

The full experience curve formula appears below. (In the formula, asterisk (*) means multiply, caret (^) means to-the-power-of, and lg means logarithm.)

<unit cost> = <start-up unit cost> * (<cumulative volume>/<start-up volume>) ^ (lg(<experience curve slope>)/lg(2))

The unit cost is a function, f(x), where x is the cumulative volume.

f(x) = <start-up unit cost> * (x /<start-up volume>) ^ (lg(<experience curve slope>)/lg(2))

Using the example above at cumulative volumes of 1,000, 2,000, 4,000 the formulas work out like this:

f(1000) = 100 * (1000/1000) ^ (lg(.8)/lg(2))

      = 100 * 1 = 100

because one raised to any power is one.

f(2000) = 100 * (2000/1000) ^ (lg(.8)/lg(2))

      = 100 * 2 ^ (lg(.8)/lg(2)

take the log of both sides,

$$lg(f(2000)) = lg(100 * 2 \char94 (lg(.8)/lg(2))$$
$$= lg(100) + lg(2 \char94 (lg(.8)/lg(2))$$
$$= lg(100) + (lg(.8)/lg(2)) * lg(2)$$
$$= lg(100) + lg(.8)$$
$$= lg(100*.8)$$
$$lg(f(2000)) = lg (80)$$

take the inverse of the log—exponentiate both sides,

$$f(2000) = 80.$$

$$f(4000) = 100 * (4000/1000) \char94 (lg(.8)/lg(2)$$
$$= 100 * 4 \char94 (lg(.8)/lg(2)$$

take the log of both sides,

$$lg(f(4000)) = lg(100 * 4 \char94 (lg(.8)/lg(2))$$
$$= lg(100) + lg(4 \char94 (lg(.8)/lg(2))$$
$$= lg(100) + (lg(.8)/lg(2)) * lg(4)$$
$$= lg(100) + (lg(.8)/lg(2)) * lg(2*2)$$
$$= lg(100) + (lg(.8)/lg(2)) * (lg(2) + lg(2))$$
$$= lg(100) + lg(.8) + lg(.8)$$
$$= lg(100*.8*.8)$$
$$lg(f(4000)) = lg (64)$$

take the inverse of the log—exponentiate both sides,

$$f(4000) = 64.$$

Because the ratio of two logarithms is the active term, the logarithms may be either log, base 10, or ln, base e.

As the experience (cumulative volume) grows from 1,000 to 2,000 to 4,000, the unit cost diminishes from 100 to 80 to 64.

Conclusion

In this chapter we have seen how the rules of style helped to write a large new spreadsheet and to modify a large existing spreadsheet. We have also seen an example of a business explanation of a somewhat sophisticated spreadsheet model. The rules helped significantly. The spreadsheets are solid performers, capable of being modified, and clear in their explanations to the attentive reader.

7

Examples

The Model QUEST

The model QUEST helps make a decision between alternatives evaluated with several conflicting criteria for choice. Read in its entirety, QUEST provides a good example of what a model built for use and reuse might look like.

	A	B	C	D	E	F	G	H
1	QUEST 15 October 1495 King Henry							
2								
3	Pick the best land to gain glory with a quest.							
4								
5	Decide which choice best satisfies several required and desired objectives.							
6	List the choices, then list and weight the objectives to be met. Rank the choices							
7	against each other and pick the choice with the highest weighted score.							
8								
9	Reference: Kepner, Charles H., and Tregoe, Benjamin B., "The New Rational							
10	Manager," Princeton, NJ: Princeton Research Press, 1981, pp. 83–102.							
11								

(continued)

	A	B	C	D	E	F	G	H
12	Contents: (each section is a named range)							
13	INTRO	Introduction: Title, description, contents, and directions						
14	INITIAL	Initial data and beginning assumptions						
15	MODEL	Decision model						
16	GRAPH	Choice's bar graph.						
17								
18	Directions:							
19	In the initial data area:							
20	1. State the decision and the desired result.							
21	2. Put in choices and make comments.							
22	3. Enter "must" objectives—things that must be satisfied.							
23	4. Enter "want" objectives—things that you would like to have.							
24	5. Weight the importance of the "want" objectives and comment.							
25	6. Rate or rank the choices against each objective.							
26	For example, rate the best choice (of four) as 4 and let the others have 3, 2,							
27	or 1. You may have ties if you wish. You may rate a choice 0 if you wish.							
28	In the decision model:							
29	7. Examine the model's results and graph.							
30	8. Revise and re-examine the importance of objectives, the rank of choices,							
31	and other features to be sure of your choice.							
32	9. List the adverse consequences of the best choice to see if it will work.							
33								
34								

The introduction covers a lot of important ground, including a brief reference to a source that explains the full method behind the spreadsheet. The
directions give step-by-step guidance to the user.

	A	B	C	D	E	F	G	H
35	Initial data and beginning assumptions							
36								
37	DECISION AND RESULT:							
38		Pick the best land to gain glory with a quest.						
39								
40	CHOICES		COMMENTS					
41	Northumberland	Nice country, lots of dwarves.						
42	Easton	Tough country, magic rings in abundance.						
43	Southington	No known questing beast.						
44	Westerly	Good roads, friendly elves.						
45								
46	"MUST" OBJECTIVES		COMMENTS					
47	Questing Beast		A questing beast to be slain					
48	Maiden in distress		A maiden to be rescued					
49	Holy relic		A relic to bring back to the Church					
50								
51	"WANT" OBJECTIVES		IMPORTANCE AND COMMENTS					
52	Elves	10	Have magic, can be big help on quest					
53	Magic rings	10	Help in the quest					
54	Good camps	9	Water and firewood for camps					
55	Smooth roads	7	Easy to travel					
56	Golden treasures	5	Nice to find					
57	Dwarves	4	Can help on the quest					
58	Friendly castles	2	Places to stay					
59	Trolls	1	Some help with bridges					
60								

The Initial Data Area tells quite a story. The King needs to choose which of four kingdoms to explore on a quest. He needs to bring back a holy relic, needs to slay a questing beast, and he needs to rescue a maiden in distress. He would like to have the help of elves and magic rings. He would like good travel conditions. Of less importance to him are the presence of golden treasures, dwarves, friendly castles, and trolls.

The first part of the initial data is mostly text. Notice, however, that the names of the four lands can be data for some spreadsheets that allow pointing to a label. The most important feature about this first part of the Initial Data Area is that it provides room for the necessary information to be spread out and, not only identified, but commented upon where appropriate. The most important data entered here is the relative importance given to the various criteria by which the user shall evaluate the choices.

	A	B	C	D	E	F	G	H
61		North	East	South	West			
62	Questing Beast	1	1	0	1			
63	Maiden in distress	1	1	1	1			
64	Holy relic	1	1	1	0			
65								
66				Relative scores				
67	Elves	2	2	3	4			
68	Magic rings	1	4	1	4			
69	Good camps	4	1	3	2			
70	Smooth roads	1	3	2	4			
71	Golden treasures	4	3	2	1			
72	Dwarves	4	4	2	1			
73	Friendly castles	4	4	2	4			
74	Trolls	3	4	1	3			
75								

The second part of the Initial Data Area contains the real meat of the model, the cross rating of each alternative by each criteria. When the user has completed the entry of this data, the model can grind out a conclusion.

	A	B	C	D	E	F	G	H
76	Decision model							
77				CHOICES				
78	"MUST" OBJECTIVES		North	East	South	West		
79	Questing Beast		1	1	0	1		
80	Maiden in distress		1	1	1	1		
81	Holy relic		1	1	1	0		
82								Check
83	"WANT" OBJECTIVES	Importance		Weighted scores				sums
84	Elves	10	20	20	30	40		110
85	Magic rings	10	10	40	10	40		100
86	Good camps	9	36	9	27	18		90
87	Smooth roads	7	7	21	14	28		70
88	Golden treasure	5	20	15	10	5		50
89	Dwarves	4	16	16	8	4		44
90	Friendly castles	2	8	8	4	8		28
91	Trolls	1	3	4	1	3		11
92								
93		Totals	120	133	104	146		503
94								
95	First choice: Easton							
96	Adverse effects of first choice (see also relative scores in initial data area):							
97	—Be prepared for tough camping							
98	—Try to stay at castles as much as possible							
99	—Double check on Westerly's lack of a holy relic.							
100	--							

The model evaluates the data collected in the Initial Data Area and illustrates, in this case, which alternative should be chosen: Easton. (Two of our alternatives failed one or more of the "must" objectives.) The model includes a check-sum column to allow a cross check of the results. Beneath the arithmetic of the model is a written summary of the adverse consequences of the first choice. Note that one of the items in the list is a reminder to double check on the existence of a relic in Westerly. If Westerly could pass that "must" objective, it would be the most preferred choice.

	A	B	C	D	E	F	G	H
101	Choice's bar graph:							
102								
103	Northumberland	120						
104	Easton	133						
105	Southington	104						
106	Westerly	146						
107	--							

The Graph Area compactly collects the data for display. The bottom two choices are valid, and the top two are invalid because they failed a "must" criteria. The graph itself visually reinforces how important it is to be sure that Westerly is disqualified. It is the clear winner of the "want" criteria rating.

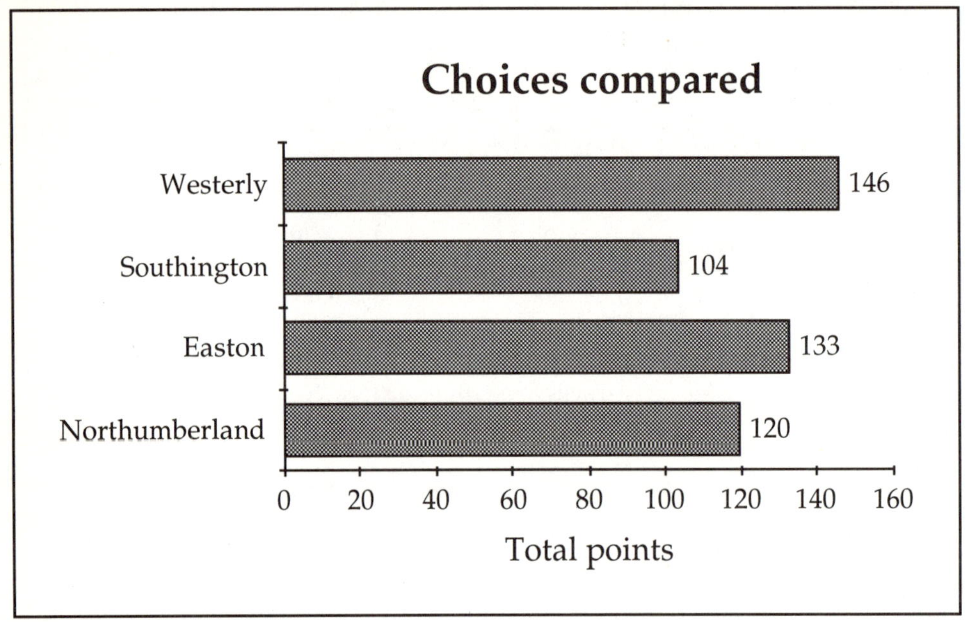

Figure 7-1.

QUEST shows how the parts of the basic form can reinforce one another. The Introduction tells you quickly what is going on and that directions exist where you need them. The Initial Data Area supports and elaborates on the Introduction with concrete data and explanatory comments. The Initial Data Area makes it easy for a new user to ask "what if" questions with this model. Finally, the directions make it possible for a new user not only to modify the present model, but to completely revise it to make a new decision. The next model, LADY, illustrates a version the Queen developed to choose a new lady in waiting.

The Model LADY

Queen Elizabeth wanted a new lady in waiting with diplomatic talents. She had had some success in modifying other tools of her husband to suit her own needs, so she renamed a version of QUEST and set to work. The first thing she did was set down her goal and re-examine the introduction to alter any other details. Because most of the introduction was a generic description, she quickly completed the initial work.

	A	B	C	D	E	F	G	H
1	LADY 16 November 1495 Queen Elizabeth of York							
2								
3	Choose a lady in waiting who will have diplomatic talents.							
4								
5	Decide which choice best satisfies several required and desired objectives.							
6	List the choices, then list and weight the objectives to be met. Rank the choices							
7	against each other and pick the choice with the highest weighted score.							
8								
9	Reference: Kepner, Charles H., and Tregoe, Benjamin B., "The New Rational							
10	Manager," Princeton, NJ: Princeton Research Press, 1981, pp. 83–102.							
11								
12	Contents: (each section is a named range)							
13	INTRO Introduction: Title, description, contents, and directions							
14	INITIAL Initial data and beginning assumptions							
15	MODEL Decision model							
16	GRAPH Choice's bar graph.							
17								
18	Directions:							
19	In the initial comments area:							
20	1. State the decision and the desired result.							
21	In the initial assumptions area:							
22	2. Put in choices and make comments.							
23	3. Enter "must" objectives—things that must be satisfied.							
24	4. Enter "want" objectives—things that you would like to have.							
25	5. Weight the importance of the "want" objectives and comment.							
26	6. Rate or rank the choices against each objective.							
27	For example, rate the best choice (of four) as 4 and let the others have 3,							
28	2, or 1. You may have ties if you wish. You may rate a choice 0 if you wish.							
29	In the decision model:							
30	7. Examine the model's results and graph.							
31	8. Revise and re-examine the importance of objectives, the rank of choices,							
32	and other features to be sure of your choice.							
33	9. List the adverse consequences of the best choice to see if it will work.							
34								
35	---							

Because the model was new to her, the Queen spent a good deal of time going over the fundamental rules to be sure she understood how to use it herself. She read the "must" objectives and the "want" objectives and spent a good deal of time making and revising her own list for her lady in waiting. She also spent considerable time deciding who the likely candidates were. When she had completed her homework, she entered her results in the first part of the Initial Data Area.

	A	B	C	D	E	F	G	H
36	Initial data and beginning assumptions							
37								
38	DECISION AND RESULT:							
39		Choose a lady in waiting who will have diplomatic talents.						
40								
41	CHOICES		COMMENTS					
42	Jane	Beautiful, English, skilled at music, wealthy family.						
43	Kate	English, of good family, skilled at poetry.						
44	Anne	Stunning, skilled in languages, French, poor family.						
45	Mary	German, wealthy family, exquisite manners.						
46								
47	"MUST" OBJECTIVES		COMMENTS					
48	Noble blood		To be a lady at court, she must be from a noble family.					
49	Speaks English		She must speak English fluently (if she is from					
50			the continent).					
51								
52	"WANT" OBJECTIVES		IMPORTANCE AND COMMENTS					
53	Good looks	10	To be effective, she must be stunning.					
54	Money	9	She should bring money when she comes to court.					
55	Spanish	7	Able to understand important visitors.					
56	French	7	Able to understand important visitors.					
57	Table manners	6	Because so many gatherings are around meals.					
58	Music	4	Able to play an instrument, sing, and dance.					
59	Poetry	4	Accomplishment becoming a lady.					
60	Needlework	1	A skill I must say I considered, but do not value highly.					
61								

Her four choices were two English ladies, Jane and Kate, French Anne, and German Mary. Each had her own accomplishments.

Her "must objectives" had to include noble blood and fluent English. Nobility was required for her to gain access to the influential lords. They did not care whether a lady was of high or low nobility, but she could not, by custom, be admitted to their social affairs if not of pedigreed birth. Fluency in English was an absolute requirement for a person who would be used to influence diplomatic gatherings. The subtle shades of the language must be understood. Of course it was also desirable to be fluent in other languages for similar reasons.

Among her "want" criteria, good looks was the only traditional feminine virtue to be of much value. Money and ability with languages accounted for more than the traditional accomplishments of a lady. Traditional accomplishments, however, could not be wholly ignored, and together they might outweigh some of the more sober virtues.

The next part was hard for the Queen. She rated and rerated her four choices on her 10 criteria. Two were easy, but the eight "want" objectives were time-consuming. After several tries she was finally satisfied she had done as much as she could to get it right.

	A	B	C	D	E	F	G	H
62		Jane	Kate	Anne	Mary			
63	Noble blood	1	1	1	1			
64	Speaks English	1	1	1	1			
65								
66				Relative scores				
67	Good looks	3	3	4	2			
68	Money	3	2	1	4			
69	Spanish	2	0	4	2			
70	French	4	4	4	0			
71	Table manners	1	3	4	4			
72	Music	4	2	2	2			
73	Poetry	1	4	3	2			
74	Needlework	3	3	4	1			
75								

All four passed the muster of the "must" criteria. Among the other criteria, Jane was the poorest, but the most beautiful, Mary, the richest, but plain, Jane and Kate were in between. French Anne, however, was a master of several languages—at least among the four choices she was the strongest in Spanish and French. The four's skills in traditional accomplishments were varied.

The Queen examined the results of her evaluation with great interest.

	A	B	C	D	E	F	G	H
76	Decision model							
77				CHOICES				
78	"MUST" OBJECTIVES		Jane	Kate	Anne	Mary		
79	Noble blood		1	1	1	1		
80	Speaks English		1	1	1	1		
81								
82	"WANT" OBJECTIVES	Importance		Weighted scores				Checksums
83	Good looks	10	30	30	40	20		120
84	Money	9	27	18	9	36		90
85	Spanish	7	14	0	28	14		56
86	French	7	28	28	28	0		84
87	Table manners	6	6	18	24	24		72
88	Music	4	16	8	8	8		40
89	Poetry	4	4	16	12	8		40
90	Needlework	1	3	3	4	1		11
91								
92		Totals	128	121	153	111		513
93								

French Anne won hands down. The checksum column was clear, so no errors had crept into her reworking of her husband's model. Anne won on her looks, her language skills, and her better than average mastery of the traditional accomplishments of a lady. The Queen studied the results for a while to be sure she had been fair to each candidate. Then she made a list of the adverse consequences of her first choice.

	A	B	C	D	E	F	G	H
94	Adverse effects of first choice (see also relative scores in initial data area):							
95	—Lady Anne will not bring a strong dowry to court.							
96	—This means that the treasury will be poorer than anticipated this year.							
97	—Must find another means of raising some money.							
98								
99	---							

The Queen knew how to deal with raising money. In order to secure the approval of her husband, she followed his example and graphed the results of LADY.

	A	B	C	D	E	F	G	H
100	Choice's bar graph:							
101								
102	Jane	128						
103	Kate	121						
104	Anne	153						
105	Mary	111						
106								

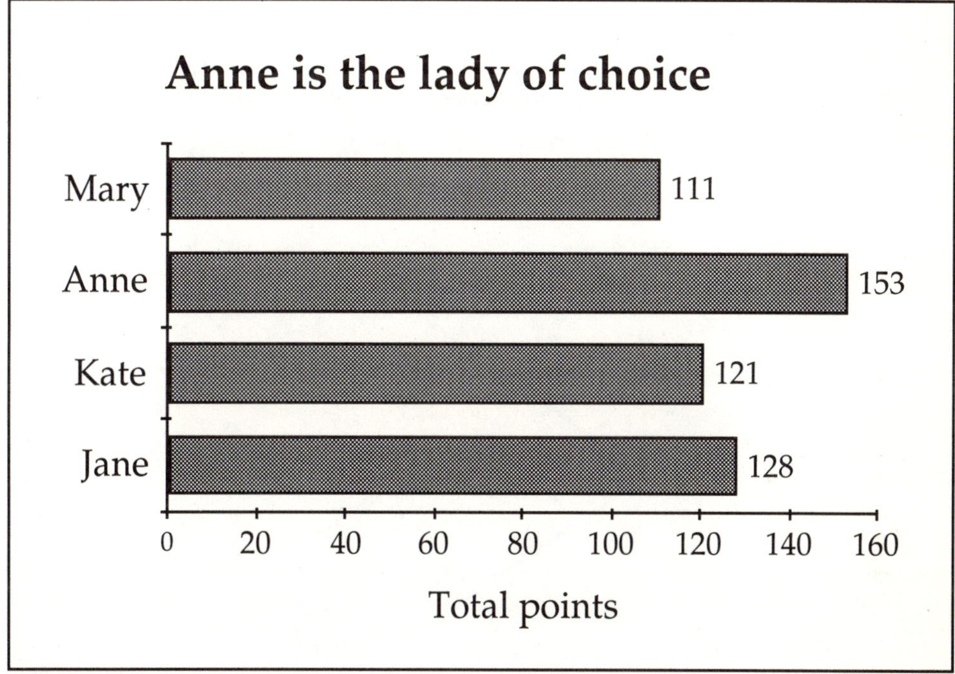

Figure 7-2.

The King gave his approval. As the original author, he was pleased that the Queen had used his model to such good effect. He understood her decision and could explain it to the English fathers of Jane and Kate. The Queen offered Anne the job as her new lady is waiting. Anne was a huge success.

The Model RAINCOAT

Sometimes while using a spreadsheet such as QUEST to arrive at a decision, the decision maker needs additional help to assess the adverse future consequences of an alternative. Sometimes the future remains uncertain. The next two spreadsheets, RAINCOAT and PIETEST, can help you assess the consequences of an uncertain future and make decisions under this uncertainty.

The classic problem of uncertain future is the weather. The classic decision made under this uncertainty is whether to wear a raincoat on a cloudy day. The cloudy day is important. Notice it is not a rainy day. You don't know whether or not it will rain. As a matter of fact, the weather forecast is a 50 percent chance of rain.

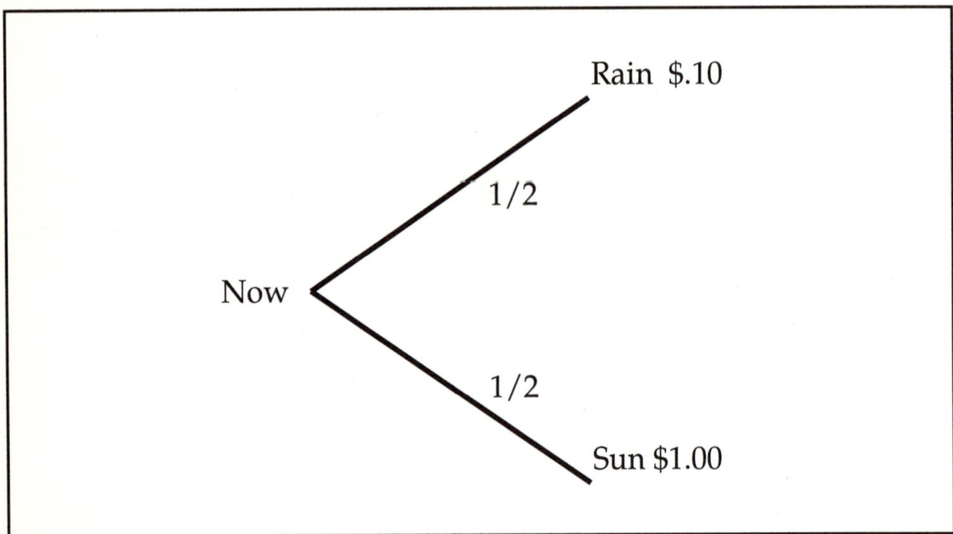

Figure 7-3.

The cloudy day represents nature's uncertain future. Figure 7-3 is one way of diagramming the predicament. If you were to get a dime when it rained and a dollar when the sun came out, then the expected value of the situation is the total of the reward times the chance of getting the reward; that is:

$$\text{Expected value} = (1/2) * 10 + (1/2) * 100$$

$$= 55$$

If the weather forecast is only a one-third chance of rain, the odds in this game would change and the expected value would change as well:

Expected value $= (1/3) * 10 + (2/3) * 100$

$$= 70$$

Notice that as the odds shift toward a favorable outcome, the expected value of the forecast goes up. This is only common sense.

The reason this chance game of nature is important is that it will influence your decision. Suppose for a moment that having a raincoat when it rains pleased you 10 points; having to carry your raincoat when the sun shines displeased you −20 points; not having a raincoat when it rains displeased you −50 points; and not having your raincoat on a sunny day pleased you 80 points.

With values for the possible outcomes, you are ready to make your decision in the face of the weather's uncertainty. You could diagram your situation as in Figure 7-4.

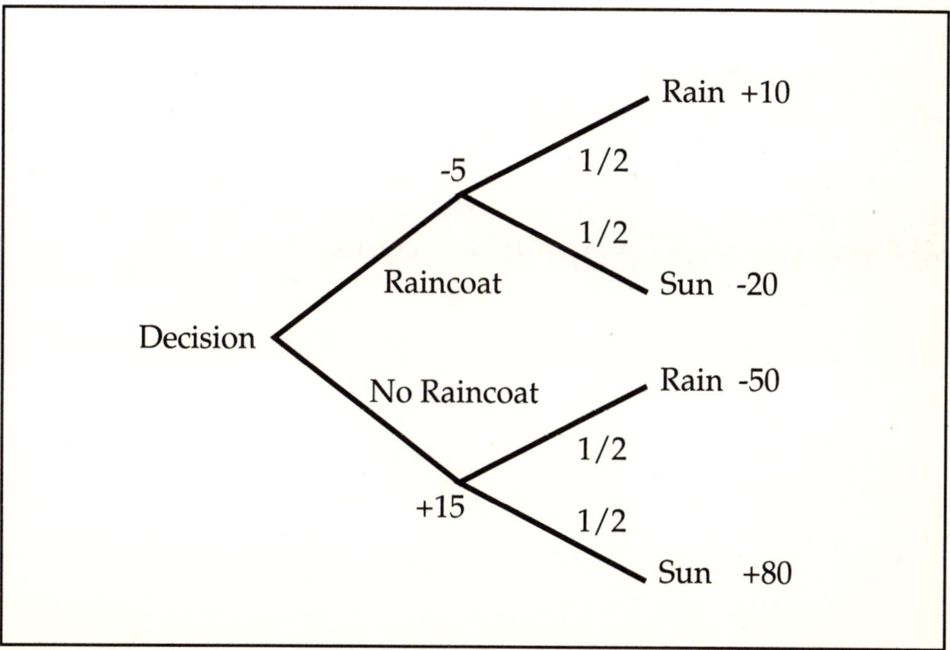

Figure 7-4.

Your must decide between two different plays of nature's game. The reason for the two plays is that the outcomes have different values:

Raincoat Game = (1/2) * 10 + (1/2) * -20

$$= -5$$

No raincoat game = (1/2) * –50 + (1/2) * 80

$$= 15$$

Fifteen points is better than -5, so you choose not to take a raincoat when the forecast is only a 50 percent chance of rain.

Notice that you could repeat the evaluation of chancy situations for different alternatives with different payoff criteria and use the results of these various games of nature to fill in values in the decision table of QUEST or LADY.

The table might be:

	Raincoat	*No Raincoat*
First person's criteria	–5	15
Second person's values	XX	XX
Third person's values	YY	YY

You could fill in the table with the results of different payoffs others might have for the same uncertain futures. The model RAINCOAT allows you to see this decision played out in front of your eyes.

	A	B	C	D	E	F	G	H
1	RAINCOAT 30 Dec 1988 J. M. Nevison							
2								
3	25-Feb-89 :Date printed							
4	(C) Copyright 1988 by John M. Nevison							
5								
6	Show how the raincoat decision can be represented as a tree.							
7								
8	Reference: John M. Nevison, "1-2-3 Spreadsheet Design"							
9	New York, NY: Brady Books, 1989.							
10								
11	Contents: (each section is a named range in 1-2-3)							
12	INTRO Introduction: Title, description, contents							
13	INITIAL Initial data and beginning assumptions							
14	MODEL Decision tree							
15	--							
16	Initial data and beginning assumptions							
17								
18	50.0% Chance of rain							
19	50.0% Chance of sun							
20	Outcome payoffs							
21	10 Wear raincoat and it rains							
22	-20 Wear raincoat and the sun shines							
23	-50 No raincoat and it rains							
24	80 No raincoat and the sun shines							
25	--							
26	Decision tree							
27	Tricky formulas:							
28	value of decision = maximum of (alternatives)							
29	value of chance game = sum of (chance of outcome * value of outcome)							
30								
31		Decision		Chance games		Primary outcomes		
32						(* indicates end of branch)		
33		15 Decision		-5 Raincoat	50%	10 *Rain		
34					50%	-20 *Sun		
35								
36				15 No raincoat	50%	-50 *Rain		
37					50%	80 *Sun		
38	==							

The Initial Data Area clearly distinguishes what you must know at the beginning: the chance of rain, and how you value the various outcomes. Should the chance of rain change, or should your feeling about the payoffs change, you may quickly revise your model.

The model itself calculates from right to left to allow the reader to progress from left to right, from final answer back to initial conditions. The reader is free to browse through as many or as few details as necessary to understand the result. The ends of the branches of the decision tree are indicated with an asterisk (*).

One interesting experiment you can conduct with this model is to alter the chance of rain to find out at what percentage your outcome payoffs are evenly balanced (in this case, it's a 62.5 percent chance of rain).

	A	B	C	D	E	F	G	H
16	Initial data and beginning assumptions							
17								
18	62.5%	Chance of rain						
19	37.5%	Chance of sun						
20	Outcome payoffs							
21	10	Wear raincoat and it rains						
22	-20	Wear raincoat and the sun shines						
23	-50	No raincoat and it rains						
24	80	No raincoat and the sun shines						
25	--							
26	Decision tree							
27	Tricky formulas:							
28	value of decision = maximum of (alternatives)							
29	value of chance game = sum of (chance of outcome * value of outcome)							
30								
31		Decision		Chance games		Primary outcomes		
32						(* indicates end of branch)		
33	-1.25 Decision			-1 Raincoat	63%	10 *Rain		
34					38%	-20 *Sun		
35								
36				-1 No raincoat	63%	-50 *Rain		
37					38%	80 *Sun		
38	==							

The Model PIETEST

A more elaborate problem with different kinds of uncertainty was faced by the Pieman whom Simple Simon met. The Pieman wanted to bring to market a new kind of pie. He figured there was a 75 percent chance folks would like it and a 25 percent chance they would not. If it failed, he would lose 50 ducats of materials and time from his current business of 200 ducats. If it succeeded he would add 80 ducats of new profit to his current business.

The simple decision looks easy.

	C	D	E	F	G	H	I
37	247.5	No test	247.5	Release	75%	280	*Like
38			200	*Continue	25%	150	*Don't like

The game has a value of 247.5 versus a stand pat decision of 200. The Pieman should decide to release the new pie into production. But what if the Pieman has the chance to do a little market research?

A market test will consist of a friend walking about the market place and asking customers if they would like the new pie. The friend will charge only 2 ducats and the Pieman is convinced he will know with 90 percent certainty whether or not the market likes his new idea. Should he conduct the market test?

The decision trees for what he would find out look like this.

	F	G	H	I	J	K	L
31	267	Like	267	Release	90%	280	*Like
32		Decision	200	*Continue	10%	150	*Don't like
33							
34	200	Don`t like	163	Release	10%	280	*Like
35		Decision	200	*Continue	90%	150	*Don't like

These trees, assembled with his previous knowledge, gather into a decision that looks like this.

	A	B	C	D	E	F	G	H	I	J	K	L
31	250.25	Decision	250.25	Test	75%	267	Like	267	Release	90%	280	*Like
32							Decision	200	*Continue	10%	150	*Don't like
33												
34					25%	200	Don't like	163	Release	10%	280	*Like
35							Decision	200	*Continue	90%	150	*Don't like
36												
37			247.5	No test	247.5	Release		75%	280	*Like		
38					200	*Continue		25%	150	*Don't like		
39												
40	==											

The Pieman sees that the value of the test is 2.75 ducats and decides to pay his friend 2 ducats to conduct a market test. If the friend had charged 3 ducats, the Pieman would have declined doing the test.

The full spreadsheet looks like this.

	A	B	C	D	E	F	G	H	I	J	K	L
1	PIETEST 30 December 1620 P. Pieman											
2												
3	25-Feb-89 :Date printed											
4	(C) Copyright 1988 by John M. Nevison											
5												
6	Evaluate a decision to pay for some market research.											
7												
8	Reference: John M. Nevison, "1-2-3 Spreadsheet Design,"											
9	New York, NY: Brady Books, 1989.											
10												
11	Contents: (each section is a named range in 1-2-3)											
12	INTRO Introduction: Title, description, contents											
13	INITIAL Initial data and beginning assumptions											
14	MODEL Decision tree											
15	--											
16	Initial data and beginning assumptions											
17	75% Chance market will like new product											
18	25% Chance market will hate new product											
19	90% Test certainty											
20	Payoff structure											
21	280 Value if market likes new product											
22	150 Value if market hates new product											
23	200 Value if present product is continued											
24	--											
25	Decision tree											
26	Tricky formulas:											
27	value of decision = maximum of (alternatives)											
28	value of chance game = sum of (chance of outcome * value of outcome)											
29	(* indicates end of branch)											
30												
31	250.25	Decision	250.25	Test	75%	267	Like	267	Release	90%	280	*Like
32							Decision	200	*Continue	10%	150	*Don't like
33												
34					25%	200	Don't like	163	Release	10%	280	*Like
35							Decision	200	*Continue	90%	150	*Don't like
36												
37			247.5	No test	247.5	Release		75%	280	*Like		
38					200	*Continue		25%	150	*Don't like		
39												
40	==											

The Model SEASON

When figures vary on a regular basis over the course of a year, a common way to look for the trend in the data is to seasonally adjust the figures. When you try to look beyond the last known figure, often you fit a line through the seasonally adjusted points and figure the next month off the line. Sometimes the figure is unadjusted to find out what next month's actual result is predicted to be. The model SEASON does just that. Its result is a graph, shown in Figure 7-5.

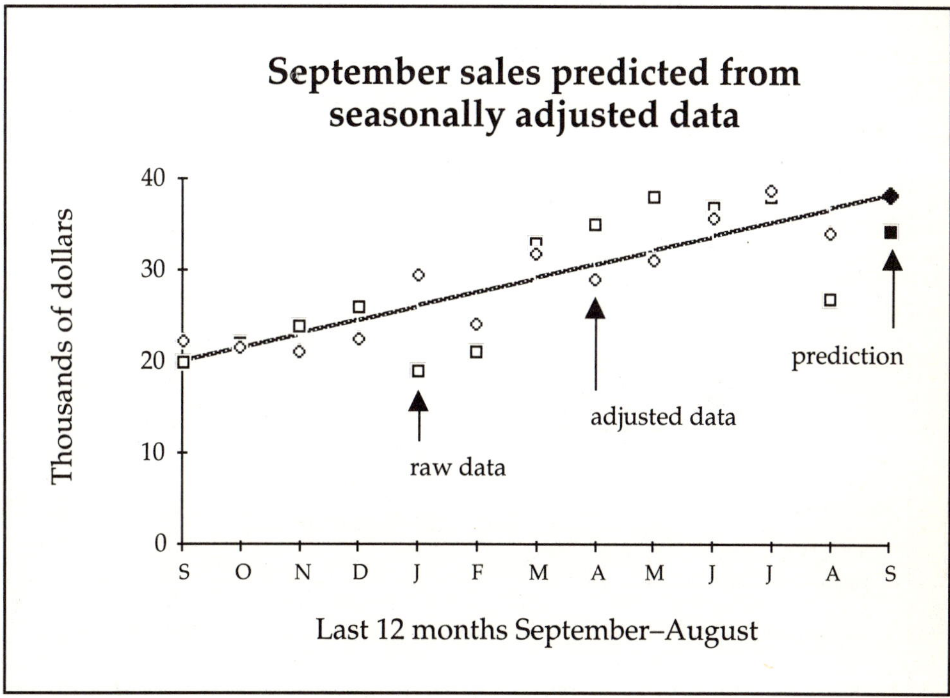

Figure 7-5.

The result of SEASON contains the raw data of the last 12 months, the seasonally adjusted data, the best-fit line and the projections for next month's figure. If you look closely at the raw data you will see that it fluctuates over the year.

This fluctuation is confirmed by the seasonal factors that are computed from the four back years of data.

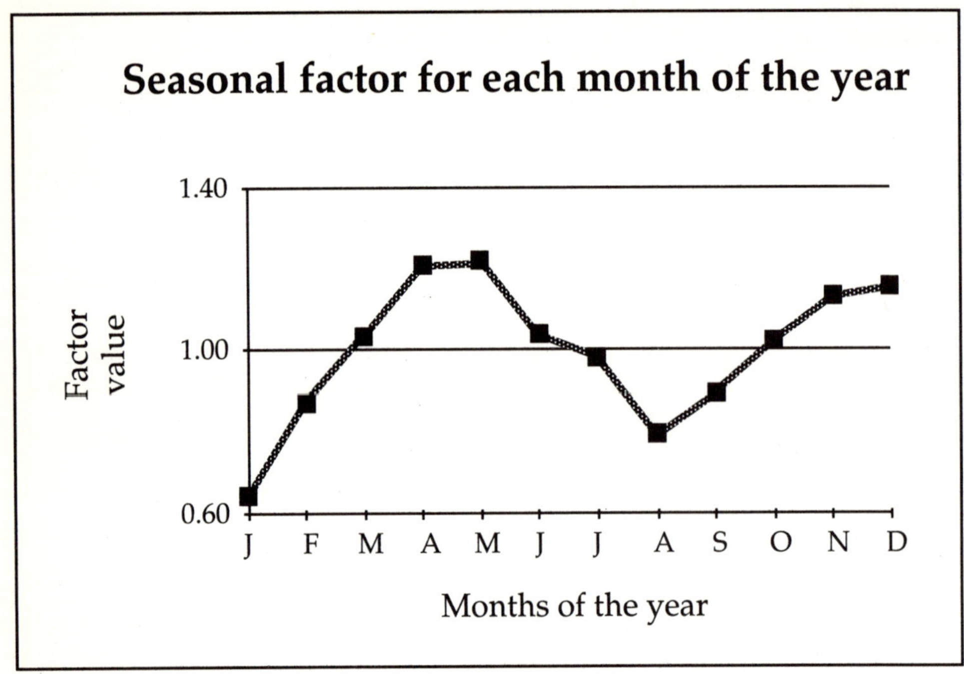

Figure 7-6.

The year begins low and works to a high in April, declines through the summer, then rises toward a second high in December. The seasonal effect is pronounced.

The spreadsheet SEASON starts off with no surprises.

	A	B	C	D	E	F	G	H	I	J	K	L
1	SEASON 28 August 1640 J. Sprat											
2												
3	Predict next month's figure by using a best-fit line through											
4	adjusted data. The seasonal adjustment is made using factors											
5	that are computed from four prior years of monthly data.											
6												
7	Contents: (each section is a named range)											
8	INTRO Introduction: Title, description, contents											
9	INITIAL Initial data and beginning assumptions											
10	MODEL Model											
11			Seasonal factors									
12			Project next month's figure									
13	GRAPH Graph area											
14	--											
15	Initial data and beginning assumptions											
16		1Yr	2Yr	3Yr	4Yr		This year					
17	January	10	10	12	15		19					
18	February	14	15	17	17		21					
19	March	16	19	19	21		33					
20	April	18	20	23	27		35					
21	May	20	21	22	25		38					
22	June	16	20	19	20		37					
23	July	15	19	18	19		38					
24	August	13	15	15	14		27					
25	September	11	17	18	20							
26	October	13	20	20	22							
27	November	14	22	23	24							
28	December	15	21	23	26							
29	--											

The Introduction and the Initial Data Area together quickly locate the reader and show him or her that the Model Area will do its work in two parts. The initial data shows four back year's data and the first part of the current year.

		Raw Monthly Data				Monthly Factors				Seasonal
30	Model Seasonal factors									
31										
32	Tricky formulas:									
33	Monthly factor = <raw monthly factor>/<average raw yearly factor>									
34	Seasonal factor = average(four monthly factors)									
35										
36		Raw Monthly Data				Monthly Factors				Seasonal
37		1Yr	2Yr	3Yr	4Yr	1Yr	2Yr	3Yr	4Yr	Factors
38	January	10	10	12	15	0.69	0.55	0.63	0.72	0.65
39	February	14	15	17	17	0.96	0.82	0.89	0.82	0.87
40	March	16	19	19	21	1.10	1.04	1.00	1.01	1.04
41	April	18	20	23	27	1.23	1.10	1.21	1.30	1.21
42	May	20	21	22	25	1.37	1.15	1.15	1.20	1.22
43	June	16	20	19	20	1.10	1.10	1.00	0.96	1.04
44	July	15	19	18	19	1.03	1.04	0.94	0.91	0.98
45	August	13	15	15	14	0.89	0.82	0.79	0.67	0.79
46	September	11	17	18	20	0.75	0.93	0.94	0.96	0.90
47	October	13	20	20	22	0.89	1.10	1.05	1.06	1.02
48	November	14	22	23	24	0.96	1.21	1.21	1.15	1.13
49	December	15	21	23	26	1.03	1.15	1.21	1.25	1.16
50										
51	Average	14.6	18.3	19.1	20.8	1.00	1.00	1.00	1.00	1.00
52										

The first part of the Model Area computes the seasonal factors. The two
tricky formulas are presented first, followed by the calculations laid out
from leftmost initial data to rightmost final result. The reader can methodi-
cally step across the page and follow the calculations at each step. Every
factor column reiterates its formula in the bottom "Average" row where the
correct answer 1.00 reassures the reader that the calculation is, in fact, correct.

After calculating the seasonal factors, the model turns its attention to pro-
jecting next month's figure.

	A	B	C	D	E	F	G	H	I	J	K	L
53	Project next month's figure											
54			The 12 months begin in September.									
55												
56	Fit a line to a set of points (x(i),s(i)), where each s(i) is the seasonally adjusted											
57	version of y(i). Use the line to predict the succeeding point, s(13), and seasonally											
58	adjust it to find y(13).											
59												
60	(For details on the line-fitting calculation see the model LINEFIT in											
61	"Executive Computing: How to get it done with Spreadsheets and Graphs," by											
62	John M. Nevison, Atlanta, GA: AMCEE, 1986.)											
63												
64	Tricky formulas:											
65	s(i) = y(i)/<seasonal factor for month>											
66	Each x' = x(i) - average x(i)											
67	Each s' = s(i) - average s(i)											
68	Slope of line, M = sum(x'*s')/sum(x'*x')											
69	Intercept of line, B = <average s(i)> - M * <average x(i)>											
70	Best fit line = M * x(i) + B											
71	Seasonally adjusted predicted month = M * 13 + B											
72	Raw predicted month = <seasonally adjusted predicted month> *											
73					<seasonal factor for month>								
74												Best
75				Seasonal				Calculations					Fit
76		x(i)	y(i)	Fctrs	s(i)			x'	s'	x'*s'	x'*x'		Line
77	September	1	20	0.90	22.3			-5.5	-6.2	33.91	30.25		20.1
78	October	2	22.	1.02	21.5			-4.5	-6.9	31.26	20.25		21.6
79	November	3	24	1.13	21.2			-3.5	-7.2	25.30	12.25		23.1
80	December	4	26	1.16	22.5			-2.5	-6.0	15.01	6.25		24.6
81	January	5	19	0.65	29.4			-1.5	1.0	-1.46	2.25		26.2
82	February	6	21	0.87	24.1			-0.5	-4.4	2.19	0.25		27.7
83	March	7	33	1.04	31.9			0.5	3.4	1.71	0.25		29.2
84	April	8	35	1.21	29.0			1.5	0.5	0.78	2.25		30.7
85	May	9	38	1.22	31.2			2.5	2.7	6.81	6.25		32.3
86	June	10	37	1.04	35.7			3.5	7.2	25.27	12.25		33.8
87	July	11	38	0.98	38.7			4.5	10.3	46.22	20.25		35.3
88	August	12	27	0.79	34.1			5.5	5.6	30.80	30.25		36.8
89	----------	---------	---------	---------	---------	------				---------	---------		
90	Average	6.5			28.5			Sums		217.8	143.0		
91											1.52	= M	
92											18.56	= B	
93	Equation :	y =	1.52 * x +		18.56								
94	Seasonally adjusted predicted month:											
95		x =	13		y =	38.4							
96	Predicted month:											
97			34.4	0.90	Seasonal factor							
98	--											

This part begins with some words of introduction followed by another set of tricky formulas. The deeper explanation of the computations is deferred to a formal reference, but the details of what the formulas are is revealed in the model. The numbers are arranged, again, in a left to right progression across the page, arriving at the coordinates of the best-fit line on the right edge.

Below the first pass of calculations, the details of the predicted month, Month 13, unfold. The predicted point on the line is 38.4, and the seasonally unadjusted figure is 34.4.

After the model has finished its computational work, it must arrange its results in a way convenient to graph.

	A	B	C	D	E	F	G	H	I	J	K	L
99	Graphing section:											
100	1. "Next month's sales"											
101	2. "Seasonal factors"											
102	Next month's sales							Seasonal factors				
103	x-label	x(i)	y(i)	s(i)	Line	s(13)	y(13)	x-label				
104	S	1	20	22.3	20.1			J	0.65	1		
105	O	2	22	21.5	21.6			F	0.87	1		
106	N	3	24	21.2	23.1			M	1.04	1		
107	D	4	26	22.5	24.6			A	1.21	1		
108	J	5	19	29.4	26.2			M	1.22	1		
109	F	6	21	24.1	27.7			J	1.04	1		
110	M	7	33	31.9	29.2			J	0.98	1		
111	A	8	35	29.0	30.7			A	0.79	1		
112	M	9	38	31.2	32.3			S	0.90	1		
113	J	10	37	35.7	33.8			O	1.02	1		
114	J	11	38	38.7	35.3			N	1.13	1		
115	A	12	27	34.1	36.8			D	1.16	1		
116	S	13			38.4	38.4	34.4					
117	==											

The Graph Area takes advantage of its space to list the graphs by name, to set up a column of labels for the graph of the most recent 12 months, to reserve special columns for s(13) and y(13) , and a column of all ones to draw a line through the center of a set of factors. Exactly how each of these columns works is unimportant. What is important is that the Graph Area allows the author enough room, so that he or she can create exactly the right graph. The graph remains the most important point of this spreadsheet.

The Model TASKTIME

When a planner gets several chores lined up and looks at the uncertainty associated with any one of these, it may seem as if the whole project is in real danger of never getting done. Actually, just the opposite is true, if you can estimate the parts of a job well, the composite whole is easier to estimate. In the spreadsheet TASKTIME, King Henry puts together a model to help him estimate the length of time it might take to gain control of a neighboring kingdom.

The beginning of the spreadsheet introduces the reader to the method employed.

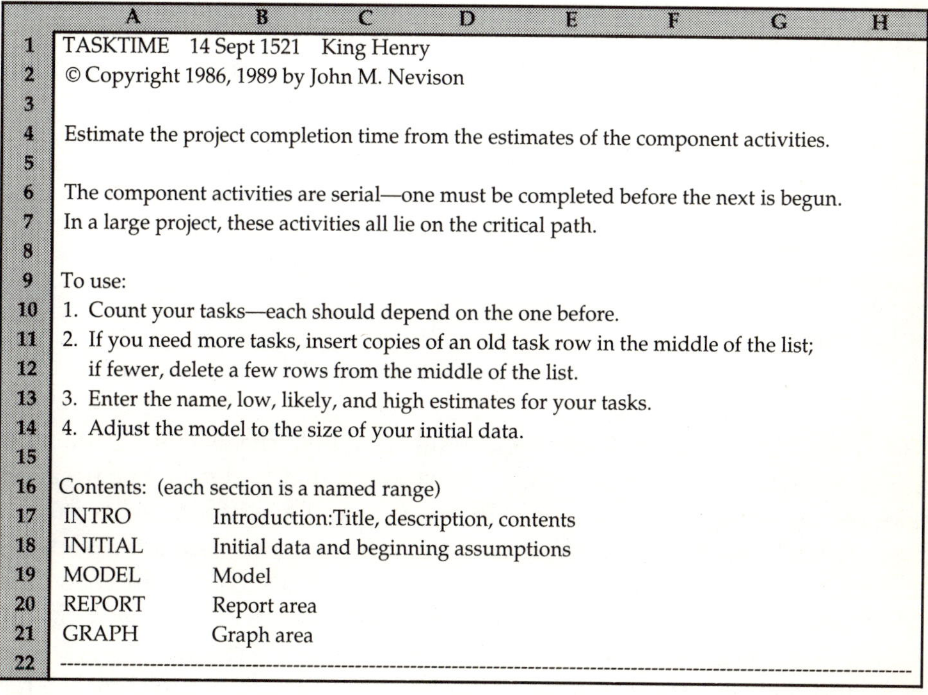

	A	B	C	D	E	F	G	H
1	TASKTIME 14 Sept 1521 King Henry							
2	© Copyright 1986, 1989 by John M. Nevison							
3								
4	Estimate the project completion time from the estimates of the component activities.							
5								
6	The component activities are serial—one must be completed before the next is begun.							
7	In a large project, these activities all lie on the critical path.							
8								
9	To use:							
10	1. Count your tasks—each should depend on the one before.							
11	2. If you need more tasks, insert copies of an old task row in the middle of the list;							
12	if fewer, delete a few rows from the middle of the list.							
13	3. Enter the name, low, likely, and high estimates for your tasks.							
14	4. Adjust the model to the size of your initial data.							
15								
16	Contents: (each section is a named range)							
17	INTRO		Introduction:Title, description, contents					
18	INITIAL		Initial data and beginning assumptions					
19	MODEL		Model					
20	REPORT		Report area					
21	GRAPH		Graph area					
22	--							

The instructions emphasize the requirement that the tasks follow one another and that each depends on the one before. Two sets of tasks that have these properties are the tasks on a critical path of a large project and the tasks you, as an individual, set out to do on any given day. (Many times some of the personal tasks may be independent, but if they all must be finished by one person, the set's time requirements behave as if the individual tasks were serially dependent.)

	A	B	C	D	E	F	G	H
23	Initial data and beginning assumptions							
24	-Low has a 1/1000 chance of happening—very optimistic estimate,							
25	everything goes right.							
26	-High has a 1/1000 chance of happening—extremely pessimistic estimate,							
27	everything goes completely wrong.							
28	-Likely is the most likely single estimate (the mode),							
29	everything is completely normal.							
30								
31	Task name		Low	Likely	High			
32	Make nails		8	10	20			
33	Make shoes		5	15	30			
34	Shoe horses		4	8	15			
35	Train riders		5	10	25			
36	Win battles		21	35	180			
37	Gain kingdom		20	30	60			
38	--							

The Initial Data Area has some reminders that help the user enter the right kind of estimates for each task. King Henry estimated his tasks. The first two make use of his blacksmith shop. He must make nails before he can make shoes. After the manufacturing is complete the same smithy must shoe all the horses. If his cousin can learn the job and work a second shift each day, and if his cousin is good, the job will proceed quickly; if either get sick, the job will be slowed. Because of the new shoes, the riders must train themselves and their mounts for battle. Winning a battle involves finding the foe and engaging him (victory is assumed). Whether the foe stands and fights or runs and must be cornered leads to great uncertainty in the time it will take to conclude a major victory in battle. The formalities of assuming the crown could be done in three weeks, but if the ceremonies must stand on the attendance of certain visiting royalty, then it might be delayed several weeks.

When he had finished entering the initial data, the King turned his attention to the model itself.

	A	B	C	D	E	F	G	H
39	Model							
40	Tricky formulas:							
41	Expected = (low + 4*likely + high)/6							
42	Standard deviation = (high - low)/6							
43	Variance = (standard deviation)^2							
44	Project standard deviation = square root (project variance)							
45								
46	Task name	Low	Likely	High	Expected	Variance		
47	Make nails	8	10	20	11.3	4.0		
48	Make shoes	5	15	30	15.8	17.4		
49	Shoe horses	4	8	15	8.5	3.4		
50	Train riders	5	10	25	11.7	11.1		
51	Win battles	21	35	180	56.8	702.3		
52	Gain kingdom	20	30	60	33.3	44.4		
53							Standard deviation	
54	Project totals				137.5	782.5	28.0	
55	Check sums	63	108	330	137.5			
56	--							

The model itself begins with a list of the tricky formulas employed in the calculations. With that help the King can see how his individual task estimates were combined into an estimate for the whole project. He examines the results closely because he doesn't believe it should take so long. After reviewing the individual tasks, confirming to himself that the individual tasks could not be doubled up, and reviewing how this project compared to the last one like it, he decides the estimate is accurate.

He checks his old Report Area and Graph Area to see if they still work.

	A	B	C	D	E	F	G	H
57	Report area							
58	26-Nov-40	ESTIMATED PROJECT COMPLETION TIME						
59								
60	6	Number of activities on the project critical path						
61	137.5	Project mean completion time (50–50 chance)						
62	28.0	Project completion time standard deviation						
63								
64			PROJECT COMPLETION TIME TABLE					
65	Time:	54	102	114	123	131	138	
66	Probability:	~0%	10%	20%	30%	40%	50%	
67								
68	Time:	138	144	152	161	173	221	
69	Probability:	50%	60%	70%	80%	90%	~100%	
70								
71	--							
72	Graph area							
73	"Timely's completion time": the project probable completion time							
74		Std. devs	Curve	Prob.	Times			
75		-3.00	0.02	0.1%	54	54		
76		-2.50	0.07	0.6%				
77		-2.00	0.21	2.3%				
78		-1.50	0.51	6.7%	96	96		
79		-1.00	0.95	15.9%				
80		-0.50	1.39	30.9%				
81		0.00	1.57	50.0%	138	138		
82		0.50	1.39	69.1%				
83		1.00	0.95	84.1%				
84		1.50	0.51	93.3%	179	179		
85		2.00	0.21	97.7%				
86		2.50	0.07	99.4%				
87		3.00	0.02	99.9%	221	221		
88	==							

After he looks at them for a few minutes he remembers that they both depend on only three numbers from the Model Area: the number of tasks, the project mean, and project standard deviation. The answers appear to be correct.

Finally he calls up the graph called "Project's probable completion time."

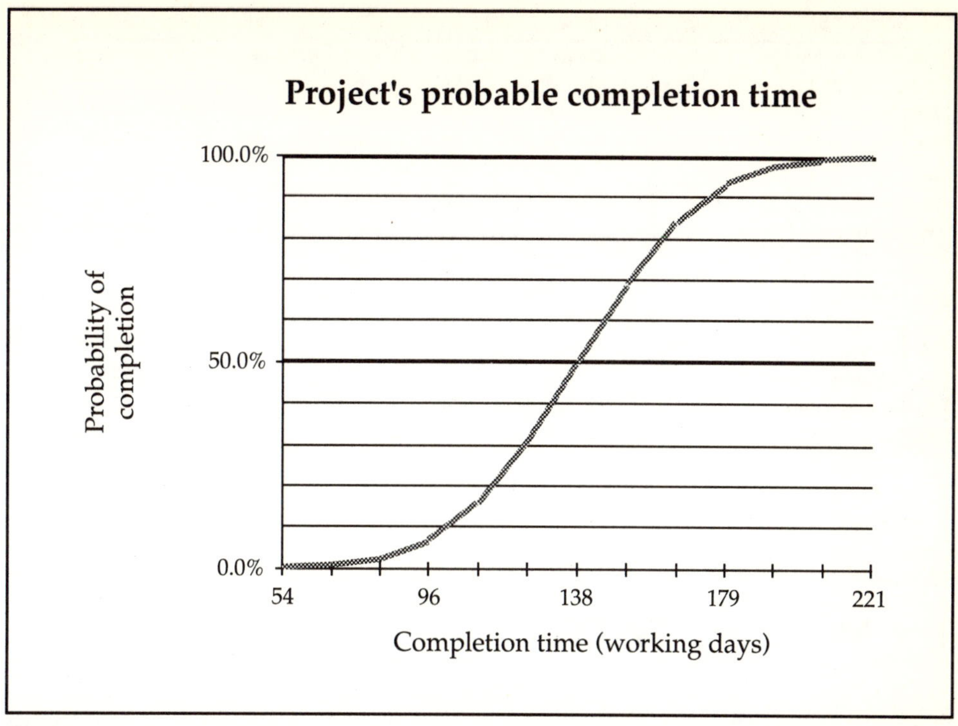

Figure 7-7.

The curve tells him the campaign will be over in four to six months. The model tells him the campaign's completion depends heavily on how fast he can engage the enemy. After he prints out copies for his files, he saves a copy of the model for later adjustment as the project unfolds.

To save a general tool that he can use later on another project, the King enters an appropriate set of initial test data and checks the model to be sure it correctly manipulates the test data.

	A	B	C	D	E	F	G	H
50	Task name	Low	Likely	High	Expected	Variance		
51	Activity 1	2	5	14	6.0	4.0		
52	Activity 2	2	5	14	6.0	4.0		
53	Activity 3	2	5	14	6.0	4.0		
54	Activity 4	2	5	14	6.0	4.0		
55	Activity 5	2	5	14	6.0	4.0		
56	Activity 6	2	5	14	6.0	4.0		
57	Activity 7	2	5	14	6.0	4.0		
58	Activity 8	2	5	14	6.0	4.0		
59	Activity 9	2	5	14	6.0	4.0		
60							Standard deviation	
61	Project totals				54.0	36.0	6.0	
62	Check sums	18	45	126	54.0			
63	--							

The answers are correct. He saves this version of the model for his next project and goes to bed.

The Model ACTIVITY

This model tracks a project's many activities as they are opened and closed through the different phases of the project. A discussion of most of the model appears in Chapter 2, and a discussion of the graphing portion appears in Chapter 4. The whole model is included here to make it easy to find for future reference.

	A	B	C	D	E	F	G	H	I	J	K	L	M	N	O	P	Q
1	ACTIVITY (Project Activity Tracking) 3 January 1520 T. Tittlemouse																
2																	
3	25-Feb-89 :Date printed																
4	(C) Copyright 1985 by John M. Nevison																
5																	
6	Track the number of assigned activities during a project.																
7	The project is to build a new catapult.																
8																	
9	To use:																
10	1. Enter the new weekly data in the Initial Data.																
11	2. Examine the model																
12	3. Print the graphs.																
13																	
14	Contents: (each section is a named range)																
15	INTRO			Introduction: Title, description, contents													
16	INITIAL			Initial data and beginning assumptions													
17	MODEL			Quarterly model													
18	GRAPH			Graphing area													
19	VERIFY			Verify area													
20	---																
21	Initial data and beginning assumptions																
22			Activities as they occured														
23	Week number	1	2	3	4	5	6	7	8	9	10	11	12	13	14	15	16
24	Design activities																
25	Assigned	5	6	7	7	7	8	7	6	6	5	4	4	3	3	3	2
26	Completed	0	3	4	5	6	7	7	6	5	4	5	6	5	4	4	4
27	Build activities																
28	Assigned	0	0	0	0	0	0	3	4	5	4	4	5	6	7	5	6
29	Completed	0	0	0	0	0	0	0	2	4	5	4	5	5	6	6	4
30	Test activities																
31	Assigned	0	0	0	0	0	0	0	0	0	0	0	0	0	0	0	0
32	Completed	0	0	0	0	0	0	0	0	0	0	0	0	0	0	0	0
33	---																

	R	S	T	U	V	W	X	Y	Z	AA	AB	AC	AD	AE	AF	AG	AH	AI	AJ	AK
23	17	18	19	20	21	22	23	24	25	26	27	28	29	30	31	32	33	34	35	36
24																				
25	2	1	0	0	0	0	0	0	0	0	0	0	0	0	0	0	0	0	0	0
26	3	3	3	2	0	0	0	0	0	0	0	0	0	0	0	0	0	0	0	0
27																				
28	7	7	7	8	7	6	6	5	4	4	3	3	3	2	2	1	0	0	0	0
29	4	5	6	7	7	6	5	4	5	6	5	4	4	4	0	4	4	3	0	0
30																				
31	2	3	3	3	4	3	2	3	3	3	3	4	4	3	3	2	2	4	2	2
32	0	0	1	3	3	2	2	2	2	2	3	4	2	2	2	2	2	3	2	2
33	---	---	---	---	---	---	---	---	---	---	---	---	---	---	---	---	---	---	---	---

	AL	AM	AN	AO	AP	AQ	AR	AS	AT	AU	AV	AW	AX	AY	AZ	BA
23	37	38	39	40	41	42	43	44	45	46	47	48	49	50	51	52
24																
25	0	0	0	0	0	0	0	0	0	0	0	0	0	0	0	0
26	0	0	0	0	0	0	0	0	0	0	0	0	0	0	0	0
27																
28	0	0	0	0	0	0	0	0	0	0	0	0	0	0	0	0
29	0	0	0	0	0	0	0	0	0	0	0	0	0	0	0	0
30																
31	0	2	2	1	0	0	0	0	0	0	0	0	0	0	0	0
32	2	4	5	5	4	1	1	0	0	0	0	0	0	0	0	0
33	---	---	---	---	---	---	---	---	---	---	---	---	---	---	---	---

	A	B	C	D	E	F	G	H	I	J	K	L	M	N	O	P	Q
34	Quarterly model																
35	THE CATAPULT PROJECT: activities completed in early autumn.																
36	1520																
37		Qtr 1		Otr 2		Otr 3		Qtr 4		Total			Date: 3 January 1521				
38	Design activities																
39	Assigned	75		11		0		0		86							
40	Completed	63		23		0		0		86							
41	Build activities																
42	Assigned	31		79		14		0		124							
43	Completed	25		71		28		0		124							
44	Test activities																
45	Assigned	0		29		33		1		63							
46	Completed	0		17		35		11		63							
47																	
48	Total activities																
49	Assigned	106		119		47		1		273							
50	Completed	88		111		63		11		273							
51	--																
52	Graphing area																
53																	
54	Graphs include:																
55	1. "Catapult project activities (actual)"																
56	2. "Total activity"																
57	Cumulative counts																
58	Week number	1	2	3	4	5	6	7	8	9	10	11	12	13	14	15	16
59	Design activities																
60	Assigned	5	11	18	25	32	40	47	53	59	64	68	72	75	78	81	83
61	Completed	0	3	7	12	18	25	32	38	43	47	52	58	63	67	71	75
62	Build activities																
63	Assigned	0	0	0	0	0	0	3	7	12	16	20	25	31	38	43	49
64	Completed	0	0	0	0	0	0	0	2	6	11	15	20	25	31	37	41
65	Test activities																
66	Assigned	0	0	0	0	0	0	0	0	0	0	0	0	0	0	0	0
67	Completed	0	0	0	0	0	0	0	0	0	0	0	0	0	0	0	0
68	Total activities																
69	Assigned	5	11	18	25	32	40	50	60	71	80	88	97	106	116	124	132
70	Completed	0	3	7	12	18	25	32	40	49	58	67	78	88	98	108	116
71																	
72																	
73	Open activities																
74	Week axis label	0	1	2	3	4	5	6	7	8	9	10	11	12	13	14	15
75	Design	0	5	8	11	13	14	15	15	15	16	17	16	14	12	11	10
76	Build	0	0	0	0	0	0	0	3	5	6	5	5	5	6	7	6
77	Test	0	0	0	0	0	0	0	0	0	0	0	0	0	0	0	0
78																	
79	Total (check)	0	5	8	11	13	14	15	18	20	22	22	21	19	18	18	16
80																	
81	--																

	R	S	T	U	V	W	X	Y	Z	AA	AB	AC	AD	AE	AF	AG	AH	AI	AJ	AK
58	17	18	19	20	21	22	23	24	25	26	27	28	29	30	31	32	33	34	35	36
59																				
60	85	86	86	86	86	86	86	86	86	86	86	86	86	86	86	86	86	86	86	86
61	78	81	84	86	86	86	86	86	86	86	86	86	86	86	86	86	86	86	86	86
62																				
63	56	63	70	78	85	91	97	102	106	110	113	116	119	121	123	124	124	124	124	124
64	45	50	56	63	70	76	81	85	90	96	101	105	109	113	113	117	121	124	124	124
65																				
66	2	5	8	11	15	18	20	23	26	29	32	36	40	43	46	48	50	54	56	58
67	0	0	1	4	7	9	11	13	15	17	20	24	26	28	30	32	34	37	39	41
68																				
69	143	154	164	175	186	195	203	211	218	225	231	238	245	250	255	258	260	264	266	268
70	123	131	141	153	163	171	178	184	191	199	207	215	221	227	229	235	241	247	249	251
71																				
72																				
73																				
74	16	17	18	19	20	21	22	23	24	25	26	27	28	29	30	31	32	33	34	35
75	8	7	5	2	0	0	0	0	0	0	0	0	0	0	0	0	0	0	0	0
76	8	11	13	14	15	15	15	16	17	16	14	12	11	10	8	10	7	3	0	0
77	0	2	5	7	7	8	9	9	10	11	12	12	12	14	15	16	16	16	17	17
78																				
79	16	20	23	23	22	23	24	25	27	27	26	24	23	24	23	26	23	19	17	17
80																				
81	---

	AL	AM	AN	AO	AP	AQ	AR	AS	AT	AU	AV	AW	AX	AY	AZ	BA
58	37	38	39	40	41	42	43	44	45	46	47	48	49	50	51	52
59																
60	86	86	86	86	86	86	86	86	86	86	86	86	86	86	86	86
61	86	86	86	86	86	86	86	86	86	86	86	86	86	86	86	86
62																
63	124	124	124	124	124	124	124	124	124	124	124	124	124	124	124	124
64	124	124	124	124	124	124	124	124	124	124	124	124	124	124	124	124
65																
66	58	60	62	63	63	63	63	63	63	63	63	63	63	63	63	63
67	43	47	52	57	61	62	63	63	63	63	63	63	63	63	63	63
68																
69	268	270	272	273	273	273	273	273	273	273	273	273	273	273	273	273
70	253	257	262	267	271	272	273	273	273	273	273	273	273	273	273	273
71																
72																
73																
74	36	37	38	39	40	41	42	43	44	45	46	47	48	49	50	51
75	0	0	0	0	0	0	0	0	0	0	0	0	0	0	0	0
76	0	0	0	0	0	0	0	0	0	0	0	0	0	0	0	0
77	17	15	13	10	6	2	1	0	0	0	0	0	0	0	0	0
78																
79	17	15	13	10	6	2	1	0	0	0	0	0	0	0	0	0
80																
81	---															

	A	B	C	D	E	F	G	H	I	J	K	L	M	N	O	P	Q
82	Verify area																
83			1302	The model verification sum													
84																	
85	If an error appears here check below and then the appropriate area of the model.																
86	(Be sure you have recalculated the whole model.)																
87																	
88			273	The total completed activities in the Model Area													
89			86	The design completed cumulative check in week 52 in the Graph Area													
90			124	The build completed cumulative check in week 52 in the Graph Area													
91			63	The test completed cumulative check in week 52 in the Graph Area													
92			756	A sum of the check totals in the Graph Area.													
93			==														

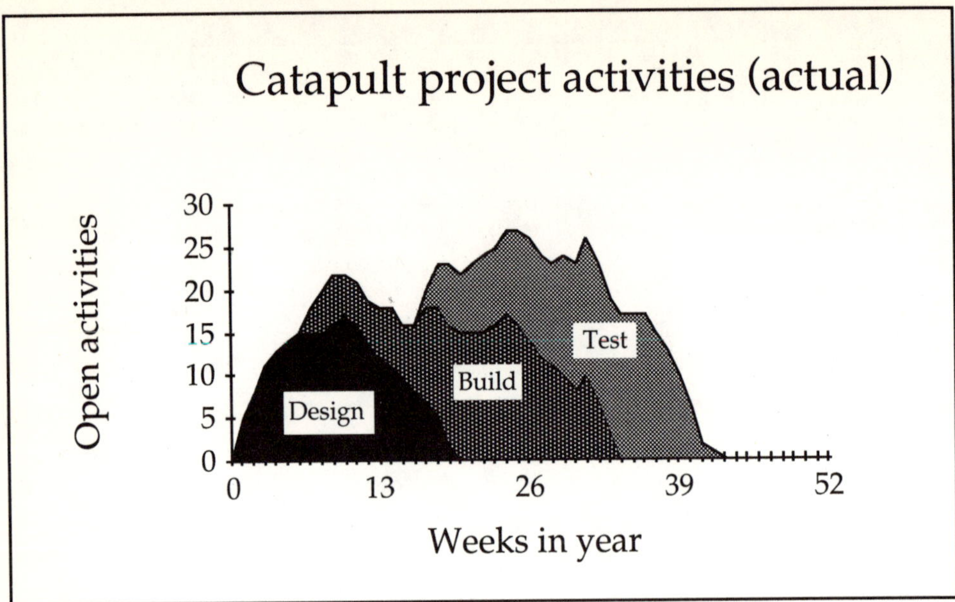

The Model PRESENT

Sometimes a spreadsheet can be an excellent tool for explaining an idea to a colleague or a business associate. PRESENT exists to explain how discounted cash flow works. Discounted cash flow allows you to evaluate and compare different business deals that involve future sums of money. To understand the spreadsheet you need a little bit of background.

Present Value

The fundamental idea behind this spreadsheet is the present value of money. Money today is worth more than money tomorrow. To convince yourself of this, ask whether you would like to receive a million dollars now, or one year from now. After a second's thought you would say now because you know you can earn interest on your money. The million now would be worth a million and some interest in a year.

People who work with money every day calculate this interest with a short cut that gets the answer in a single step. When they calculate interest, say 7 percent on $100, they multiply the $100 by a factor of 1.07 to get $107. An interest factor for a 15 percent interest rate is 1.15, while an interest factor for 3% is 1.03. In your problem with the million dollars, let I be the interest factor. The future value, F, is equal to the present value, P, times the interest factor, I.

<future value> = <present value> * <interest factor>

$$F = P * I$$

$$1{,}070{,}000 = 1{,}000{,}000 * 1.07 \text{ (if the interest rate is 7\%)}$$

Not only do you have a way of computing one year's interest, you can quickly extend your use of factors to cover several years. Here is what your million dollars would look like in three years.

<future value> = <present value> * <int. factor> * <int. factor> * <int. factor>

$$F = P * I * I * I$$

$$1{,}225{,}043 = 1{,}000{,}000 * 1.07 * 1.07 * 1.07$$

or,

$$F = P * I^3$$

$$1{,}225{,}043 = 1{,}000{,}000 * (1.07)^3 \text{ (for those who remember exponents).}$$

To find out what the future value is, we continue to multiply by interest factors until we get to the right year.

You turn future value on its head to get present value. Ask yourself another question. How much would you accept right now in lieu of getting a million dollars in one year? The answer is—whatever amount would yield a million after a year's interest. The answer, the present value (P), times the interest factor (I), would be $1,000,000, if the interest rate is 7 percent,

<amount you accept now> * <interest factor> = <million at the end of the year>

<present value> * <interest factor> = <future value>

$$P * I = \$1{,}000{,}000$$

$$P * 1.07 = \$1{,}000{,}000$$

$$P = \$1{,}000{,}000 * (1/1.07)$$

$$P = \$1{,}000{,}000 * .93457943$$

$$P = \$934{,}579.43$$

So we would accept $934,579.43 now because we know that at the end of the year we would have a million dollars. This answer depended on the number (1/1.07), or about .935, the discount factor (D), associated with a 7 percent interest rate.

$$\langle\text{discount factor}\rangle = (1/\langle\text{interest factor}\rangle)$$

$$D = (1/I)$$

$$.935 = (1/1.07)$$

The discount factor works in a similar fashion to the interest factor for several years. What is the present value of a million dollars three years from now? It's a million dollars times the discount factor three times.

$$\langle\text{pres. value}\rangle = \langle\text{million in 3 years}\rangle * \langle\text{dis. factor}\rangle * \langle\text{dis. factor}\rangle * \langle\text{dis. factor}\rangle$$

$$\langle\text{pres. value}\rangle = \langle\text{future value}\rangle * \langle\text{dis. factor}\rangle * \langle\text{dis. factor}\rangle * \langle\text{dis. factor}\rangle$$

$$P = F * D * D * D$$

$$817{,}400 = 1{,}000{,}000 * .935 * .935 * .935$$

or

$$P = F * D^3$$

$$817{,}400 = 1{,}000{,}000 * .935^3$$

The present value of a future amount is that future amount times the discount factor for however many years it takes to get back to the present.

Now we are in a position to understand all the entries in the Initial Data Area of the spreadsheet. The interest rate yields the interest factor and the discount factor. The stream of future cash flows is entered just as it occurs.

Most business deals have differing amounts of money arriving at different times. This stream of cash payments, the **cash flow**, is irregular, so no simple formula will work on it. For example, two different apartment houses have different purchase prices, different kinds of major repairs needed in the near future (one a furnace, the other a new roof), and different rent schedules for the future (and different laws in different towns governing when the rents may be increased). Which is the best buy? To decide this question you first need to estimate what the future stream of cash payments is for each apartment house. After you compute the two streams of cash flows, you will notice that they are irregular in time and different in amounts.

Table 7-1.   Two apartment investments with two different cash flows.

Year	Apartment A	Apartment B	
0	-10,000	-10,000	(Purchase)
1	2,000	1,000	(Rents–expenses)
2	3,000	2,000	
3	5,000	3,000	
4	5,000	4,000	
5	8,000	15,000	(Sale)

To decide which is the best deal, you must now discount each year's cash flow back to its present value and add up all the present values. This answer is the **net present value** of the **discounted cash flow**.

	A	B	C	D	E	F	G
1	PRESENT 5 Feb 1989 J. M. Nevison						
2							
3	26-Feb-89 :Date printed						
4	(C) Copyright 1988 by John M. Nevison						
5							
6	Illustrate how to calculate the net present value of a series of future						
7	payments. If the result is positive, then the investment is a good one.						
8							
9	Reference: John M. Nevison, "1-2-3 Spreadsheet Design,"						
10	New York, NY: Brady Books, 1989.						
11							
12	Contents: (each section is a named range in 1-2-3)						
13	INTRO Introduction: Title, description, contents						
14	INITIAL Initial data and beginning assumptions						
15	MODEL Model						
16	--						
17	Initial data and beginning assumptions						
18	10% The company cost of capital (or the inflation rate)						
19	1.10 Cost of capital factor (= 1 + cost of capital)						
20	0.91 Discount factor (= 1/(cost of capital factor)						
21							

(continued)

	A	B	C	D	E	F	G
22	YEAR	PAYMENT					
23	0	($10,000)					
24	1	2,000					
25	2	3,000					
26	3	5,000					
27	4	5,000					
28	5	8,000					
29							
30	Model						
31	Tricky formulas:						
32	This year's factor = last year's factor * discount factor						
33							
34	10%	The company cost of capital (or the inflation rate)					
35	0.91	Discount factor (= 1/(cost of capital factor)					
36							
37		Cash	Discount	Present			
38	Year	Payment	Factor	Value			
39	0	(10,000)	1.00	($10,000)			
40	1	2,000	0.91	1,818			
41	2	3,000	0.83	2,479			
42	3	5,000	0.75	3,757			
43	4	5,000	0.68	3,415			
44	5	8,000	0.62	4,967			
45							
46	Totals	13,000		6,437			
47	===						

The first stream of numbers in our spreadsheet shows a net present value of $6,437. This means your $10,000 invested in Apartment House A will yield future amounts totaling $16,437. When you plug in the numbers for Apartment House B you get a different present value.

	A	B	C	D	E	F	G
30	Model						
31	Tricky formulas:						
32	This year's factor = last year's factor * discount factor						
33							
34		10%	The company cost of capital (or the inflation rate)				
35		0.91	Discount factor (= 1/(cost of capital factor)				
36							
37			Cash	Discount	Present		
38		Year	Payment	Factor	Value		
39		0	(10,000)	1.00	($10,000)		
40		1	1,000	0.91	909		
41		2	2,000	0.83	1,653		
42		3	3,000	0.75	2,254		
43		4	4,000	0.68	2,732		
44		5	15,000	0.62	9,314		
45							
46		Totals	15,000		6,682		
47	===						

The net present value for this apartment house is $6,862. So you can use the net present value to compare two very different business deals and decide that Apartment House B is a better deal.

Notice in the spreadsheet that the interest rate is called the "corporate cost of capital." If you are using this spreadsheet for a private calculation you would want to use the inflation rate. However, if you are a corporation with stock that is traded and bonds that you have borrowed, then you have a corporate cost of capital that you would want to use to determine your discount rate. Details on how to calculate this rate can be found in Copeland and Weston in the References.

If you decide to play with the inflation rate, you can find one that balances the cost against the rewards so the net present value is 0. You will have found the internal rate of return for the deal.

	A	B	C	D	E	F	G
30	Model						
31	Tricky formulas:						
32	This year's factor = last year's factor * discount factor						
33							
34		28%	The company cost of capital (or the inflation rate)				
35		0.78	Discount factor (= 1/(cost of capital factor))				
36							
37			Cash	Discount	Present		
38		Year	Payment	Factor	Value		
39		0	(10,000)	1.00	($10,000)		
40		1	2,000	0.78	1,564		
41		2	3,000	0.61	1,835		
42		3	5,000	0.48	2,391		
43		4	5,000	0.37	1,870		
44		5	8,000	0.29	2,340		
45							
46		Totals	13,000		0		
47	==						

For the first investment, a rate of about 28 percent (really 27.871 percent) balances the cost against the reward and is the internal rate of return.

In fact, PRESENT illustrates the calculations behind several 1-2-3 functions. The calculations of net present value illustrate how the function @NPV(int,range) works. "Range" includes the series of future cash flows and "int" is the discounted periodic interest rate.

The internal rate of return can be calculated automatically by the 1-2-3 function @IRR(guess, range) where "range" is the series of cash flows, and "guess" is an initial guess at the answer. The function figures out the exact answer. The short spreadsheet PRESENTS illustrates the @IRR function and the @NPV function in action.

	A	B	C	D	E	F	G
1	PRESENTS 5 Feb 1989 J. M. Nevison						
2							
3	26-Feb-89 :Date printed						
4	(C) Copyright 1988 by John M. Nevison						
5							
6	Illustrate how to calculate the net present value (NPV) and the internal						
7	rate of return (IRR) of a series of future payments. If the NPV is						
8	positive, then the investment is a good one. This spreadsheet makes use of						
9	the 1-2-3 @NPV and @ IRR functions.						
10							
11	Reference: John M. Nevison, "1-2-3 Spreadsheet Design,"						
12	New York, NY: Brady Books, 1989.						
13							
14	Contents: (each section is a named range in 1-2-3)						
15	INTRO Introduction: Title, description, contents						
16	INITIAL Initial data and beginning assumptions						
17	MODEL Model						
18	---						
19	Initial data and beginning assumptions						
20	10% The company cost of capital (or the inflation rate)						
21							
22	YEAR PAYMENT						
23	0 ($10,000)						
24	1 2,000						
25	2 3,000						
26	3 5,000						
27	4 5,000						
28	5 8,000						
29	---						
30	Model						
31	Tricky formulas:						
32	<net present value> = @NPV<years 1-5> - <year 0>						
33							
34	10% The company cost of capital (or the inflation rate)						
35							
36	$6,437 The net present value.						
37	27.9% The internal rate of return.						
38	==						

Notice that the @NPV function works on years 1 to 5 so the formula had to subtract (or add the negative amount of) the initial year 0 payment to get the full net present value of the entire cash flow.

If you have a series of even payments, two other 1-2-3 functions, @PV(pmt,int,term) and @FV(pmt,int,term), will compute the present value or future value given the "pmt," payment, the "int," periodic interest rate, and the "term," the number of payment periods.

The Models SIMPLPAY and PAYMENTS

The next two spreadsheets also illustrate some basic financial ideas; In this case, the schedule of even loan payments that a bank loan or a mortgage loan requires for repayment. The first spreadsheet SIMPLPAY illustrates a straightforward example.

	A	B	C	D	E	F
1	SIMPLPAY 29 Nov 88 J. M. Nevison					
2	26-Feb-89 :Date printed					
3	(C) Copyright 1988 by John M. Nevison					
4						
5	Show how a payment schedule's principle percentage varies as					
6	the interest rate increases.					
7						
8	Reference: John M. Nevison, "1-2-3 Spreadsheet Design,"					
9	New York, NY: Brady Books, 1989.					
10						
11	Contents: (each section is a named range in 1-2-3)					
12	INTRO Introduction: Title, description, contents					
13	INITIAL Initial data and beginning assumptions					
14	YEARLY Yearly model					
15	VERIFY Verify area					
16	---					
17	Initial data and beginning assumptions					
18	1000.00 Amount borrowed					
19	10 Number of years					
20	10.0% Annual interest rate					
21	162.75 Yearly payment = @PMT(amount, interest rate, number of years)					
22	---					

(continued)

	A	B	C	D	E	F
23	Yearly model					
24	Tricky formulas:					
25	Interest = Beginning balance * interest rate					
26	Principal = Yearly payment - interest					
27	New beginning balance = Old beginning balance - principal					
28						
29			10.0%	Interest rate		
30			162.75	Yearly payment		
31		Beginning			Principal	
32	Year	Balance	Interest	Principal	(% of payment)	
33	1	1000.00	100.00	62.75	39%	
34	2	937.25	93.73	69.02	42%	
35	3	868.23	86.82	75.92	47%	
36	4	792.31	79.23	83.51	51%	
37	5	708.80	70.88	91.87	56%	
38	6	616.93	61.69	101.05	62%	
39	7	515.88	51.59	111.16	68%	
40	8	404.72	40.47	122.27	75%	
41	9	282.45	28.25	134.50	83%	
42	10	147.95	14.80	147.95	91%	
43						
44	Totals		627.45	1000.00		
45						
46	---					
47	Verify area					
48		1000.00	Verification sum			
49	If an error appears here, check below and then the appropriate area of					
50	the spreadsheet. (Be sure you have recalculated the whole model.)					
51						
52		1000.00	Yearly principal total cross check			
53	===					

The spreadsheet finds the amount of the periodic payment by using the 1-2-3 function @PMT(prin,int,term) where "prin" is the principal borrowed, "int" is the periodic interest rate, and "term" is the number of payment periods.

If you look at the model area, you can see that beginning with the interest rate and the even monthly payment, the spreadsheet works out how much interest is due each year, subtracts that from the payment, and applies the remaining payment against the principal of the loan to reduce the outstanding balance. This procedure is repeated each year until the loan is paid off.

The point of the spreadsheet is to illustrate what percentage of the payment is principal as the loan is being paid off. This is illustrated in the last column entitled "Principal (% of Payment)." As you can see, the first years' payments are more interest than principal; in year four, the principal becomes more than half the payment and by year 10, almost all the payment is principal. This is precisely the pattern a schedule of mortgage payments follows.

The spreadsheet uses a sum of $1,000 and a rate of 10 percent because it is easy to check that the calculations are correct. The spreadsheet also compares the sum of the principal payments and the initial sum borrowed to verify that the calculations are being done correctly.

The only shortcoming of this model is that it produces a schedule that is paid on an annual basis, not on a monthly basis. The second spreadsheet, PAYMENTS, attempts to remedy this shortcoming by producing a monthly schedule with an annual summary.

	A	B	C	D	E	F	G
1	PAYMENTS 21 Nov 88 J. M. Nevison						
2	26-Feb-89 :Date printed						
3	(C) Copyright 1988 by John M. Nevison						
4							
5	Show how a payment schedule's principle percentage varies as						
6	the interest rate increases.						
7							
8	Reference: John M. Nevison, "1-2-3 Spreadsheet Design,"						
9	New York, NY: Brady Books, 1989.						
10							
11	Contents: (each section is a named range in 1-2-3)						
12	INTRO		Introduction: Title, description, contents				
13	INITIAL		Initial data and beginning assumptions				
14	YEARLY		Yearly model				
15	MONTHLY		Monthly model				
16	VERIFY		Verify area				
17	--						
18	Initial data and beginning assumptions						
19	1000.00	Amount borrowed					
20	10	Number of years					
21	10.0%	Annual interest rate					
22	120	Number of months = 12 * number of years					
23	0.8%	Monthly interest rate = Annual rate / 12					
24	13.22	Monthly payment = @PMT(amt.,monthly int. rate,number of mo.)					
25	158.58	Yearly payment = 12 * monthly payment					
26	--						
27	Yearly model			Interest	10.0%		
28				Payment	158.58		
29		Beginning					
30	Year	Balance	Interest	Principal	Principal (%)		
31	1	1000.00	97.24	61.34	39%		
32	2	938.66	90.82	67.77	43%		
33	3	870.89	83.72	74.86	47%		
34	4	796.03	75.88	82.70	52%		
35	5	713.33	67.22	91.36	58%		
36	6	621.97	57.65	100.93	64%		
37	7	521.05	47.09	111.49	70%		
38	8	409.55	35.41	123.17	78%		

(continued)

	A	B	C	D	E	F	G
39	9	286.38	22.51	136.07	86%		
40	10	150.31	8.27	150.31	95%		
41							
42	Totals		585.81	1000.00			
43							
44	--						
45	Monthly model			Interest	0.8%		
46				Payment	13.22		
47		Beginning					
48	Month	Balance	Interest	Principal	Principal (%)		
49	1	1000.00	8.33	4.88	37%		
50	2	995.12	8.29	4.92	37%		
51	3	990.20	8.25	4.96	38%		
52	4	985.23	8.21	5.00	38%		
53	5	980.23	8.17	5.05	38%		
54	6	975.18	8.13	5.09	39%		
55	7	970.09	8.08	5.13	39%		
56	8	964.96	8.04	5.17	39%		
57	9	959.79	8.00	5.22	39%		
58	10	954.57	7.95	5.26	40%		
59	11	949.31	7.91	5.30	40%		
60	12	944.01	7.87	5.35	40%		
61	13	938.66	7.82	5.39	41%		
62	14	933.27	7.78	5.44	41%		
63	15	927.83	7.73	5.48	41%		
64	16	922.34	7.69	5.53	42%		
65	17	916.82	7.64	5.57	42%		
66	18	911.24	7.59	5.62	43%		
67	19	905.62	7.55	5.67	43%		
68	20	899.95	7.50	5.72	43%		
69	21	894.24	7.45	5.76	44%		
70	22	888.47	7.40	5.81	44%		
71	23	882.66	7.36	5.86	44%		
72	24	876.80	7.31	5.91	45%		
73	25	870.89	7.26	5.96	45%		
74	26	864.94	7.21	6.01	45%		
75	27	858.93	7.16	6.06	46%		
76	28	852.87	7.11	6.11	46%		

(continued)

About the Author

John M. Nevison is currently a senior consultant with Innovation Associates and works with major corporations on creating inspired performance.

He is the author of five books including, *The Elements of Spreadsheet Style* (Brady, 1987), and the present work. Nevison is a Phi Beta Kappa mathematics graduate of Dartmouth College. He is past Chairman of the Greater Boston Chapter of the Association For Computing Machinery.

He has been featured in articles in *The Wall Street Journal*, and his comments have appeared in *Personal Computing*, *U.S. News and World Report*, *Time*, and *Science*.

He lives with his wife and two daughters in Concord, Massachusetts.

1-2-3® Spreadsheet Design

copyright © 1989, John M. Nevison

22 Rules for Better Spreadsheet Style

1. Make a Formal Introduction

2. Title to Tell

3. Declare the Model's Purpose

4. Give Clear Instructions

5. Reference Critical Ideas

6. Map the Contents

7. Identify the Data

8. Surface and Label Every Assumption

9. Model to Explain

10. Point to the Right Source

////Brady

**Handy removable reference card. Tear along
perforations and keep by your computer.**

22 Rules for Better Spreadsheet Style

11. First Design on Paper

12. Test and Edit

13. Keep it Visible

14. Space So Spreadsheet May Be Easily Read

15. Give a New Function a New Area

16. Report to Your Reader

17. Graph to Illuminate

18. Import with Care

19. Verify Critical Work

20. Control All Macros

21. Focus the Model's Activity

22. Enter Carefully